Black Woman
and
Other Poems

Mujer Negra
y
Otros Poemas

CW00553096

Black Woman
and
Other Poems

Mujer Negra
y
Otros Poemas

by

Nancy Morejón

Translated by Jean Andrews

MANGO PUBLISHING
2001

©Nancy Morejón and Mango Publishing 2001
©Jean Andrews English Language translation and Mango Publishing 2001

First published 2001

Published by Mango Publishing, London UK
P.O. Box 13378, London SE27 OZN

ISBN 1 902294 11 4

British Library Cataloguing in Publication Data
A CIP catalogue record for this book is available from the British Library

Printed in the UK by Intype Ltd, Wimbledon

Cover design by Nancy Morejón and Jacob Ross

Introduction

The Poetry of Nancy Morejón

Nancy Morejón's first collection of poetry was published in 1962, the near world-shattering year of the Bay of Pigs stand-off between Communist East and capitalist West; her most recent emerged thirty eight years later in a very different world, where Cuba is one of only two remaining original Communist regimes. When the Cuban Revolution took place in 1959, Cuba was the 'most racist of the Hispanic Caribbean Territories'.[1] It set out as one of its chief aims the elimination of discrimination on the grounds of race and, with some caveats, has been successful in transforming Cuba into, arguably, the most racially integrated of the Caribbean nations.[2] In an essay written in 1982 on the great Cuban mulatto poet, Nicolás Guillén, Nancy Morejón put forward an optimistic and generous analysis of how the relationship between race and the moulding of national identity has been posited in post-Revolutionary Cuba, and traces the poetic parallels of such a strategy in the work of Nicolás Guillén:

> Over four centuries, a national spirit has been fashioned from cultures deposited here in diverse states: the conquistador with the common denominator of attack and power, avid for possession and adventure, the slave levelled down within the very regime of slavery. Some came to work; others came to be prisoners of work and swell the coffers of modern capitalism. Some of their own free will; others by force. Crossing the ocean was never the best of experiences for humankind and the world. And yet, the very dissociation reached conquistadors and slaves.

---

[1]   Pedro Pérez Sarduy and Jean Stubbs, 'The Rite of Social Communion' in *AfroCuba:An Anthology of Cuban Writing on Race, Politics and Culture.* Melbourne: Latin American Bureau, 1993, pp.1-33, p.9.

[2]   Catherine Davies, *A Place in the Sun:Women Writers in Twentieth-Century Cuba.* London and New Jersey: Zed Books, 1997, p.165.

Some in positions of superiority, others under the yoke of submission; all alienated, beyond themselves, in the frenetic category of transculturation.[3]

She defines transculturation, a term coined by the Cuban critic Fernando Ortiz, as a means of describing the functioning of a 'melting pot' environment in which all strands carry equal weight, thus:

Transculturation signifies constant interaction, transmutation between two or more cultural components whose unconscious end is the creation of a third cultural whole - that is, culture - new and independent, although its bases, its roots, rest on preceding elements. The reciprocal influence here is determining. No element is superimposed on the other; on the contrary, each one becomes a third entity. None remains immutable. All change and grow in a 'give and take' which engenders a new texture.[4]

She acknowledges the complexity of this interracial mix in Cuba, listing all the different cultures which constitute its heterogeneity: slaves from Senegal, Guinea, the Congo, Angola and Mozambique from tribes such as the Mandinga, Hausa, Yelofe, Dahomeyans, Yoruba; the Chinese from Macao and Canton who came in the nineteenth century; the Hispanics who held far from uniformly Castilian cultural allegiances: Andalusians, Catalans, Basques, Portuguese and Galicians, and she notes the 'total elimination from the nation's cultural panorama' of the indigenous element, wiped out by a combination of European diseases unfamiliar in the Caribbean, conquistador aggression and enforced labour. In brief, however, the two cultures of origin underpinning contemporary Cuba derive from the Spanish and the slave inheritances:

Cuban culture [...] stands out for a national awareness [which is] discovering popular roots nurtured on the ancestral wisdom of two basic components: the Hispanic

---

[3]   Ibid., 'Race and Nation', pp.227-237, p.233.
[4]   Ibid., p.229.

and the African, both of which determine our social and psychological being.[5]

This last comment is her assessment of the work of Nicolás Guillén who went a great way towards defining Cuban culture as emanating from these conjoint sources, not least by giving voice in his so-called mulatto poems to the Africanisms present in the hybridised Spanish spoken in Cuba. *The Balada de los dos abuelos*, 'Ballad of the Two Grandfathers', from his early collection, *West Indies Ltd.* (1934), in particular, describes the descent of the Cuban mulatto from an armour-clad conquistador, Don Federico, and a tambor-playing slave, Taita Facundo, one the sworn enemy of the other since African slaves were introduced to Cuba. In the poem, the speaker, Guillén, their descendent, brings about an imagined and highly significant reconciliation between them and everything they represent:[6]

> Federico!
> Facundo! The two embrace.
> The two sigh. The two
> their strong heads raise;
> the two the same size,
> under the high stars;
> the two the same size,
> black yearning and white yearning,
> the two the same size,
> they shout, they dream, they weep, they sing.
> They dream, they weep, they sing.
> They weep, they sing.
> They sing!

Nancy Morejón's is a poetry which inherits and seeks to promote this newborn wholeness; a poetry too which never fails to engage with contemporary political events and issues, and with history. The plight of black people in apartheid South Africa and the American Deep South, for example, and the U.S. invasion of the island of Grenada

---

[5]   Ibid., p.227.
[6]   Nicolás Guillén, *Songoro cosongo y otros poemas*. Madrid: Alianza Editorial, 1980, pp.27-28.

in 1983 are present in this collection, as indeed are the history of the West African slaves trafficked across the Atlantic to Cuba, the hardships of migrant workers coming from Jamaica to work in the Cuban plantations in the early twentieth century and the extreme poverty of ordinary Cuban workers down through the years. Her poetry is also imbued with an astonishing breadth and depth of cultural reference, the first among which is the complex patrimony of the Yoruba, the Ibo, the Dahomey, the Congolese and the many other tribes-people transplanted from Africa in the time of slavery, but her work also refers with deeply-read nonchalance to music, painting and literature, to figures as diverse as the French writers Blaise Cendrars and Jacques Prévert, the Italian Futurist Emilio Marinetti, Jorge Manrique and Antonio Machado, Spanish poets of very different centuries, the Cuban painters Victor Patricio de Landaluze, Marcelo Pogolotti and the lesser-known Gregorio Valdés, the nineteenth-century English engraver and map-maker, Elias Durnford and, of course, in one of her early poems, 'Richard Brought His Flute', the heterodox grouping of Mozart, Count Basie, Duke Ellington and Nat King Cole. It is part of her playfulness that all these are lightly dashed off as if they were nondescript elements of common knowledge.

Perhaps primarily, though, she celebrates, like Guillén before her, the dance, song, and music of the multifarious hybrid tradition now indigenous to Cuba. In dance, she moves from the correct and rather formal danzón adapted by slaves from European modes and popular in the nineteenth century, to the tribal dances for orishas such as Yemayá. The sounds and rhythms of traditional African instruments such as tambors and marimbulas are overtly evoked, while the son form, so beloved of her mentor, Guillén, and now no stranger to the rest of the world thanks to the phenomenal success of Ry Cooder's *Buena Vista Social Club*, is never far from the surface. Then, there is *santerismo*, a religion and way of life unique to Cuba but related to slave culture in other Latin American countries, notably Haiti and Brazil. In it, the Catholic saints imposed by the conquistadors are syncretised with tribal deities and practices salvaged, in the teeth of transportation and the slave market which was no respecter of tribal, linguistic or family allegiance, and kept alive on new soil on the plantations. All of this intertwined music, dance and ritual blossomed in the maroon, or runaway slave, communities which survived up to independence and emancipation and, as she attests, is now patrimony common, in greater and lesser measure, to all Cubans of whatever hue and ancestry.

One of Nancy's most famous and most frequently translated poems, *Mujer negra* ('Black Woman') provides both the title and the culmination to this collection of poetry. It tells the story of Cuban slavery from capture and transportation, plantation work, escape, life in the maroon communities, the fight for independence under the 'Bronze Titan', General Antonio Maceo, himself black, to the total freedom brought under Castro. It offers a counterpoint to Guillén's two grandfathers in that it is a woman's version of history, a version which, as Catherine Davies explains, was subordinated to the need to fight for racial and class equality both before and after the Revolution.[7] In fact, Davies points out that African Cuban poetry written by women was unheard of before the 1959 Revolution and even by 1970, the only woman poet included in a landmark study of African Cuban poetry by Ildefonso Pereda Valdéz was Nancy Morejón herself.[8] Matters have certainly improved since then, but it marks Nancy Morejón out as a pioneer, a lone black female voice for so many years after the dawn of the Revolution.

Yet, pioneers are apt to have their individuality overlooked, being seen instead as monoliths generally representative of all aspects of the community to which they have they just given expression. Though Nancy Morejón may be the first black Cuban woman poet, and one with a major international profile, she should also be recognised for the unique voice that she is, a poet whose work is redolent of her love of her city, her island country, its people and its Caribbean neighbours. In this collection, a delicate balance exists between those poems which engage with grand political and historical themes and the many intimate poems about family, friends, real places and places in the mind or memory. In the everyday occurrences of life, things observed and taken stock of, her eye for fine detail and profound sense of place are constantly engaged. Indeed, this filigree-work is rarely absent in the broad-brush historical and political poems either. It has evolved as her style has itself moved on, from the density of her initial, rapid-fire, expressionistic imagery to the calm and graceful, frequently nostalgic, lyricism of her later work. Indeed, her poetry, like Cuba itself, might

---

[7]   Op. Cit., pp.165ff.
[8]   Ibid., p.170–172.

be said to trace its roots equally to Jorge Manrique or Antonio Machado on the one hand and the music of tambor and marimbula on the other.

It is, above all, a poetry at peace with itself and the culture out of which it arises and to which it gives voice, using the words of a black woman, a Cuban woman, a remarkable individual named Nancy Morejón.

Jean Andrews

Acknowledgments

The poetry included in this bilingual collection was chosen and placed in order by Nancy Morejón herself. When I finished the first drafts of all the translations she patiently read them and suggested some amendments. She was available with unerring generosity to answer my e-mails asking questions as to the meaning of a particular word or the background to a certain place-name or historical figure and I am honoured to have worked so closely with her.

Because the poetry is so dense in historical reference, so very redolent also of its time and place, I have included an extensive glossary, a great deal of which is direct translation of Nancy's answers to my queries. Her input is initialled (NM) and my own carries my initials (JA). I am also greatly indebted to Jean Stubbs and Pedro Pérez Sarduy for the AfroCuban Glossary in their *Afrocuba: An Anthology of Cuban Writing on Race, Politics and Culture*, (Melbourne: Ocean Press, 1993, pp. 297-302), which I have referred to extensively. I must also thank my friends and colleagues, Catherine Davies, Tony Kapcia, Eduardo Guevara, Alda Goulding, Ignacio Rodríguez, Antonio Miguel Sánchez and Conrad James for diverse forms of assistance at various stages, and Joan Anim-Addo who initiated this project and has been unfailingly patient and encouraging throughout. My greatest obligation is to Nancy Morejón herself for her kindness and forbearance, and not least for her poetry.

The Translations

I have endeavoured to provide readable English translations which are as close to being word for word transpositions of the originals as the difference between English and Spanish syntax and idiom will allow. I have in no way attempted to emulate rhythm or rhyme beyond what the accident of near word-for-word translation has thrown up or produce anything approaching a poetic version of Nancy Morejón's work in English. Readers who have even a minimal command of Spanish will find it much more satisfying to read the poetry in Spanish and use the translations as a kind of easy-access dictionary. To make the Spanish as easy to follow as possible, and in the interests of accuracy, I have sometimes stretched English beyond its familiar idiomatic boundaries, to preserve the cadence or the literal meaning of a phrase. These the reader will note with no hint from me. Occasionally I have refused an obvious set phrase for set phrase equivalence, in order to retain an original metaphor. The poem *Botella al mar*, which I have translated as 'Bottle in the Sea', for example, might, more appropriately in other circumstances, have been rendered as 'Message in a Bottle'. However, that would have transposed rather than translated the original word picture. There are times, as well, when I have simply been unable to find a way of conveying the wit and wordplay in the Spanish without completely distorting the poem. For instance, the word for master in Spanish, *amo*, is also the first person of the verb to love, amo, but the poem, *Amo a mi amo*, as far as I could see, could only be translated as 'I love my Master'. This carries most of the sense but none of the pungent irony of the title. That said, all mistranslations and errors of any other sort are my responsibility entirely.

Contents

Introduction 5

La claridad/Clarity 16/17

I
Una rosa/A Rose 22/23
Mitologías/Mythologies 24/25
Un manzano de Oakland/An Apple Tree in Oakland 28/29
Freedom Now/Freedom Now 32/33
El camino de Guinea/The Way to Guinea 34/35
Farewell/Farewell 36/37
Parque central, alguna gente/Central Park, A Few People 38/39
Renacimiento/Rebirth 42/43
Abril/April 44/45
El ruiseñor y la muerte/The Nightingale and Death 46/47
Granadina/Grenadian Woman 48/49
Elegía a Maurice Bishop/Elegy for Maurice Bishop 50/51
Historia/History 56/57
Junto al golfo/By the Gulf 58/59
Historia de un pastor/The Story of a Shepherd 62/63
Baas/Baas 66/67
Soliloquio de un colono/Soliloquy of a Colonial 68/69
Aniversario/Anniversary 70/71
Ritornello/Ritornello 74/75
Cocinera/Cook 76/77
Balada de la cárcel de Robben/
The Ballad of Robben Island Gaol 78/79

Epitafio para una dama de Pretoria/
Epitaph for a Pretoria Lady 82/83
Nana silente para niños surafricanos/
Silent Lullaby for South African Children 84/85

II

Paisaje célebre/Famous Landscape 88/89
Ante un espejo/In front of a Mirror 90/91
Mujer con pescado/Woman with Fish 94/95
Marina/Marina 96/97
Dibujo/Drawing 98/99
Piedra pulida/Polished Stone 102/103
Orégano/Oregano 104/105
Botella al mar/Bottle in the Sea 106/107
Intuición/Intuition 110/111
El Tambor/The Tambor 112/113

III

Mirar adentro/Looking Inwards 118/119
Humus Inmemorial/Immemorial Humus 120/121
Saltimbanquis/Travelling Circus 122/123
Negro/Black Man 126/127
Hablando con una culebra/Speaking to a Snake 130/131
El loto y el café/The Lotus and the Coffee 132/133
Güijes/Güijes 134/135
Madrigal para cimarrones/Madrigal for Maroons 136/137
Niño con los ojos rosados/Child with Pink Eyes 138/139
Los ojos de Eleggua/The Eyes of Eleggua 140/141
Para escapar herido/In Order to Escape Wounded 144/145

Amo a mi amo/I Love My Master 146/147

La rebambaramba/The Rebambaramba 152/153

Elogio de Nieves Fresnada/Eulogy for Nieves Fresnada 156/157

Merceditas/Merceditas 160/161

Pareja negra/Black Couple 166/167

Mundos/Worlds 170/171

Madre/Mother 178/179

A la sombra de los tranvías/In the Shadow of the Trams ... 180/181

Richard trajo su flauta I, II,VIII/
Richard Brought His Flute, I, II,VIII 182/183

Restos del Coral Island/Remains of the Coral Island 190/191

Un patio de la Habana/A Patio in Havana 194/195

Pogolotti/Pogolotti 196/197

El hogar/The Home 200/201

Fábula de albañil/Fable of a Builder's Labourer 204/205

El café/Coffee 208/209

Cotorra que atraviesa Manrique/
Budgerigar Crossing Manrique 210/211

Instante/Instant 212/213

El río de Martín Pérez/The River of Martin Pérez 214/215

Persona/Person 220/221

Mujer negra/Black Woman 226/227

Glossary 232

Biographical Notes 243

LA CLARIDAD

A la manera de un poeta romántico...
Para Roberto Fernández Retamar

Cántame, pájaro que vuelas
sobre el espacio austral
que desconozco. Húndete
en mi sed de persona
y pósate en los dedos
que conforman mi mano.
Iremos a la floresta,
después que la lluvia
haya posado su cansancio
en la tarde. Después
que el sol haya alzado
su cabeza dorada
a través de las sonantes
hojas verdes.

La tarde es una sola,
en Greenwood o Almendares.
La puerta blanca de mi alcoba
se entreabre ya.
Rayos solos de luz
se cuelan desde allí,
alcanzando mis pies en reposo.

CLARITY

In the manner of a Romantic poet...
For Roberto Fernández Retamar

Sing to me, bird who flies
over the southern space
I do not know. Plunge yourself
into my person's thirst
and place yourself on the fingers
which make up my hand.
We will go to the glade,
after the rain
has placed its fatigue
on the evening. After
the sun has raised
its golden head
through the sounding
green leaves.

The evening is one and the same,
in Greenwood or Almendares.
The white door of my bedroom
is opening already.
Single rays of light
creep in from there,
reaching my feet in repose.

Qué humedad la que deja el chubasco
en el verano!
Este mediodia, que ya deja de ser
por el canto de un pájaro,
se esfuma con el tiempo.

Naces y mueres, claridad.
Nacemos y morimos
en esta isla de la borrasca.
Ven hacia mí,
ay, cántame, pájaro de Cuba,
en la frescura de la patria.

Octubre imprescindible

What humidity a shower leaves
in Summer!
This midday, which is already ceasing to be
because of the song of a bird
is vanishing with time.

You are born and you die, clarity.
We are born and we die
in this island of squalls.
Come towards me,
ay, sing to me, bird of Cuba,
in the freshness of the homeland.

Indispensable October

BLACK WOMAN AND OTHER POEMS

I

Una Rosa

Los ojos de Abel Santamaría
están en el jardín.
Mi hermano duerme bajo las semillas.
Santiago alumbra
la frescura del tiempo
que nos tocó vivir.
Un niño baila
el dulce aire de julio
en la montaña.
Alguien escucha su canción
bajo el estruendo puro
de una rosa.

Parajes de una época

A Rose

The eyes of Abel Santamaría
lie in the garden.
My brother is sleeping beneath the seeds.
Santiago lights up
the freshness of the time
which it was our turn to live.
A boy dances
the sweet air of July
in the mountain.
Someone listens to his song
beneath the pure thunder
of a rose.

Places in a Time

MITOLOGÍAS

Furias del huracán acostumbrado,
vientos misteriosos golpeando el arrecife,
palos de muerte y de coral
inundaron las bahías de la Isla
y se tragaron el aire de Camilo.

Sus pulmones fueron hélices negras
que naufragaron en un soplo,
desde donde las turbonadas de la misericordia
están girando,
como troncos de manigua varados,
enjaulados
en una eterna comandancia boreal.
Las chalupas y las bocas jadeantes
navegan por los mares
y Camilo perdido.

Habrá lluvias de octubre en su sombrero alón.
Pero, ¿dónde encontrar su barba fina,
acorralada entre esas aguas frías e imprevisibles?
¿Cómo apretar su firme mano
ebria de pensamiento y ebria de acto?
¿Dónde posar sus ojos,
aves anidadas del héroe?
Oh pueblo mío insurrecto,
tú que lo vieras nacer en el discurso
y arder en los vertiginosos ríos de la Invasión:
Para ti derribó madrigueras impías.
Oh pueblo mío de nubes.

MYTHOLOGIES

Furies of the usual hurricane,
mysterious winds beating the reef,
sticks of death and of coral
flooded the bays of the Island
and swallowed the air of Camilo.

His lungs were black helixes
which floundered in a gust,
from where the turbulences of mercy
are turning,
like washed-up swamp logs,
caged
in an eternal boreal command.
The skiffs and the panting mouths
sail the seas
and Camilo lost.

There might be October rains on his wide-brimmed hat.
But, where can his fine beard be found,
corralled in these cold and unpredictable waters?
How can his firm hand be pressed
drunk with thought and drunk with action?
Where can his eyes be rested,
nesting birds of the hero?
Oh my insurgent people,
you who saw him born in discussion
and burn in the vertiginous rivers of the Invasion:
For you he tore down impious dens.
Oh people of mine of clouds.

Oh pueblo suyo el que lo halla
con una flor silvestre,
amable,
deshojable,
lanzada a la intemperie,
sobre este mar de las mitologías.

Parajes de una época

Oh people of his which finds him
with a wild flower,
friendly,
its petals pluckable,
thrown to the elements,
on this sea of mythologies.

Places in a Time

Un Manzano de Oakland

para Angela Davis

¿Ves ese suave y firme manzano
dando sombra sobre una acera gris de Oakland?
          ¿Lo ves bien?
Cada molécula de su tronco viajó desde lo sbosques
                              de Dakota
y el lacrimoso Misurí.
Las aguas del gran lago de sal de Utah
regaron las resinas de su corteza.

¿Sabes que ese manzano fue plantado
con la tierra robada a los Rodilla-Herida
por el gobernador del estado?
¿Acaso tú conoces que su savia
se nutre con los huesos y pelos prisioneros
de San Quintín?

Fíjate en sus hojas misteriosas,
en los hilillos por donde pasa el jugo de esa savia.
          Míralo bien.
Mira bien tú la estación remota que inaugura.
Mira bien, niño del occidente norteamericano,
la copa del manzano,
más ancha aún que la misma costa del Pacífico,
la que guarda en su mejor raíz
carabelas y espectros.

AN APPLE TREE IN OAKLAND

For Angela Davis

Do you see this smooth and firm apple tree
shading a grey sidewalk in Oakland?
                    Are you looking closely?
Every molecule of its trunk travelled from the forests
                                    of Dakota
and the weepy Missouri.
The waters of the great salt lake of Utah
irrigated the resins in its bark.

Do you know that this apple tree was planted
with the earth stolen from the Wounded Knee
by the state governor?
Maybe you know that its sap
feeds on the imprisoned bones and hair
of San Quentin?

Pay attention to its mysterious leaves,
to the little threads through which the juice of that
                                    sap passes.
          Have a good look.
Look well, you, at the distant season it is inaugurating.
Have a good look, child of the North American West,
at the crown of the apple tree,
wider even than the very Pacific coast,
which keeps in its best root
caravels and spectres.

Y a ti, viajero, te dará sombra siempre,
pero detén tu marcha pesarosa ante esa sombra suya.
No olvidarás jamás que ha sido
la triste, cruel, umbrosa, la efímera morada
de múltiples cabezas negras colgando entre el follaje,
                                        incorruptibles.

Parajes de una época

And to you, traveller, it will always give you shade,
but halt your sorrowful step before that shade
                                    belonging to it.
You will never forget that it has been
the sad, cruel, shady, the ephemeral dwelling
of multiple black heads hanging amid the
                        foliage, incorruptible.

Places in a Time

Freedom Now

a la lucha de los negros en Estados Unidos

en el sur de los Estados Unidos
se fabrican ferrocarriles ganchos lámparas
ganchos pintura de uña para señoritas
cremas y helados de chocolate
tinte plateado autos edificios de propiedad horizontal
       televisores escuelas democráticas

se celebra Halloween en Estados Unidos
hay también Alabama Mississippi
      Texas
la gran Texas rubita y pedigüeña
Birmingham Virginia
      New Orléans-gargajo de los Luises con
            Mardi Gras y todo

es decir

ciudades misteriosas llenas de gente

que lincha negros y pisa cucarachas

cualquier vaca sureña exclamaría orgullosa:

"en estos tiempos de coca-cola
fuerza nuclear y conferencias internacionales
vale mucho más mi leche
que el semen de un estudiante negro."

Richard trajo su flauta

Freedom Now

to the struggle of the blacks in the United States

in the south of the United States
they manufacture trains hooks lamps
hooks nail varnish for young ladies
creams and chocolate ice creams
silver-dye cars condominiums
         televisions democratic schools

Halloween is celebrated in the United States
there are also Alabama Mississippi
         Texas
the great Texas blondish and demanding
Birmingham Virginia
New Orléans - phlegm of the Bourbons with Mardi
                      Gras and all

that is to say

mysterious cities full of people

who lynch blacks and walk on cockroaches

any Southern cow would exclaim proudly:

"in these times of Coca-Cola
nuclear power and international conferences
my milk is worth far more
than the semen of a black student."

Richard Brought his Flute

EL CAMINO DE GUINEA

Todos los arcoiris lograron desarmar a los traficantes
del golfo.
La estampida en Bissau aún resuena en el oído
del siglo.
El océano ahora vierte sus aguas sobre el primer
alabardero portugués
que inclina sus espadas, ahogado y vendido,
no más conquistador.
Un guerrillero triunfal de las colonias deshizo ya
aquel cerco
de horror y sumisión.
Rey de su pupila y de su lanza, amamanta la tierra
que lo viera nacer.
Vivificador de los combates, ordena la vida de la
independencia.
Entona con amor el canto viejo de sus abuelos.
Hombre que vas naciendo,
el camino de Guinea está reverdeciendo indetenible.

Parajes de una época

THE WAY TO GUINEA

All the rainbows managed to disarm the gulf
traffickers.
The stampede in Bissau still resonates in the ears of
the century.
The ocean now pours its waters over the first
Portuguese halberdier
who lowers his swords, drowned and sold out,
no longer a conquistador.
A triumphal warrior of the colonies already undid
that enclosure
of horror and submission.
King of his eye-pupil and his lance, he suckles the
land which saw him born.
Enlivener of battles, he orders the life of
independence.
He intones with love the old song of his grandparents.
Man who art being born,
the way to Guinea is greening over unstoppable.

Places in a Time

FAREWELL

Bajo el camino ciertamente enlutado,
allá al final del último sendero,
el jamaicano teje hoy su esperanza.
Quiere que el sol sea nuevo como una nueva vida.
Su quehacer fue constante.
Tan sólo comparable al anónimo constructor de las
                                        pirámides.
Desbrozó el monte de Kingstontown.
Limó las verandas de la aldea con su propia miseria.
Miró a las cadenas de montañas
y se dió cuenta de que Jamaica era una isla sumamente
                                        pequeña.
¿Añorar Cuba? ¿Rememorar Haití?
No, campesino, antillano malabarista del sudor,
no has de inmigrar ya más a tus tierras hermanas
para la zafra hórrida y la huelga.
Vuelve tu espalda y continúa fundando el camino
                          mejor para tu isla.
Di adiós, un adiós jamaicano.

Parajes de una época

FAREWELL

Beneath the road certainly clad in mourning,
there at the end of the last path,
the Jamaican today weaves his hope.
He wishes the sun were new like a new life.
His chores were constant.
Only comparable to the anonymous constructor of
the Pyramids.
He cleared the mountain of Kingston town.
He planed the verandas of the village with his own misery.
He looked at the mountain ranges
and realised that Jamaica was an essentially small island.
Long for Cuba? Call to mind Haiti?
No, peasant, Antillian juggler of sweat,
you don't have to immigrate any more to your brother
lands
for the horrid sugarcane harvest and to go on strike.
Turn your back and continue to lay the way better
for your island.
Say farewell, a Jamaican farewell.

Places in a Time

Parque Central, Alguna Gente

3:00 P.M.

el que atraviesa un parque en La Habana grande y
                                        floreciente
con mucha luz blanca mucha luz blanca
que hubiera enloquecido el girasol de aquelVan Gogh
con luz blanca que llena los ojos de los chinos
        de los chinos fotógrafos

el que atraviesa un parque y no comprende esa luz
                                        blanca
        se repite casi
el que no entiende de esas horas
da todos los rodeos innecesarios y todas las vueltas
alrededor del parque central de La Habana
el que atraviesa un parque con árboles sagrados
el que pasa con los ojos abiertos y cerrados
amando el golpe de la Revolución en los ojos
el golpe que se lleva en los ojos y en la cintura
el que sostiene de esa luz puede que sepa de la noche
                                        y el vino

porque en los parques y en este que es central el de
                                        La Habana
los viejos se sientan en un banco encienden un tabaco
                        se miran y conversan
de la Revolución y de Fidel
los viejos que ahora permanecen en un banco y toman
el sol y toman el sol y toman el sol

CENTRAL PARK, A FEW PEOPLE

3.00 P.M.

he who crosses a big and blooming park in Havana
with a lot of white light a lot of white light
which would have made the sunflower of that Van
                              Gogh go mad
with white light which fills the eyes of the Chinese
              of the Chinese photographers

he who crosses a park and does not understand that
                              white light
              which repeats itself almost
he who does not understand about these hours
does all the unnecessary rounds and takes all the walks
around the central park of Havana
he who crosses a park with sacred trees
he who passes with his eyes open and closed
loving the Revolutionary coup in his eyes
the coup which is carried in the eyes and around the
                              waist
he who sustains that light maybe knows about night
                              and wine

because in the parks and in this which is central the
                              one in Havana
the old men sit on a bench light a cigarette look at
each other and converse
about the Revolution and about Fidel
the old men who now remain on a bench and sun

para nadie es secreto
allá van dos hombres y una cartera vieja destartalada
una mano regordeta un grito con un sombrero gris
los viejos que se ven al lado de una estatua
del apóstol Martí en 1966 en diciembre de 1966
        acabándose el año y esperando
"el aniversario de la libertad y rindiendo homenaje a
        los mártires"
sí
a todos los hombres que murieron del pueblo y su sangre
para tomar el sol de la tarde en La Habana Cuba
        territorio libre de América
el que atraviesa en esa forma el parque este mundo la
        vejiga de la Revolución
tiene que suspirar
y andar despacio y respirar
y andar ligero y suspirar y respirar y andar despacio
y dar toda la vida

rabiosamente
        compañeros

              Parajes de una época

themselves and sun themselves and sun themselves
it is a secret to nobody
there go two men and an old beaten-up briefcase
a fleshy hand a shout with a grey hat
the old men who can be seen beside a statue
of the apostle Martí in 1966 in December of 1966
       the year finishing and waiting for
"the anniversary of liberty and paying homage to
          the martyrs"
yes
to all the men who died of the people and their blood
in order to take the evening sun in Havana Cuba
       free territory of America
he who crosses the park in that way this world the
       bladder of the Revolution
has to sigh
and walk slowly and breathe
and walk lightly and sigh and breathe and walk slowly
and give all his life

furiously
      companions

Places in a Time

RENACIMIENTO

Hija de las aguas marinas,
dormida en sus entrañas,
renazco de la pólvora
que un rifle guerrillero
esparció en la montaña
para que el mundo renaciera a su vez,
que renaciera todo el mar,
todo el polvo,
todo el polvo de Cuba.

Piedra pulida

REBIRTH

Daughter of the sea waters
asleep in their entrails,
I am reborn from the gunpowder
which a guerilla rifle
spread on the mountain
so that the world would be reborn in its turn,
that the whole sea would be reborn,
all the dust,
all the dust of Cuba.

Polished Stone

ABRIL

Esas hojas que vuelan bajo el cielo,
quieren decir la lengua de la patria.

Estas aves que aspiran
la lentitud hostil de la borrasca,

ya saben que en abril se precipitan
todas las agresiones.

Oh pueblo en que nací,
así te miro fiero, junto al mar;
este polvo que piso
será el huerto magnífico de todos.
Y si caemos otra vez
se alzarán los huesos en la arena.

Aquí están nuestras almas
en el mes imprevisto, en abril,
donde duerme la Isla como un ala.

Piedra pulida

APRIL

These leaves which fly beneath the sky,
want to say the language of the homeland.

These birds which breathe in
the hostile slowness of the squall,

already know that in April
all the aggressions precipitate.

Oh people into which I was born,
thus I look at you fierce, by the sea;
this dust on which I tread
will be the magnificent garden of all.
And if we fall once more
our bones will rise up in the sand.

Here our souls are
in the unforeseen month, in April.
where the Island sleeps like a wing.

Polished Stone

El Ruiseñor y la Muerte

Si voy a morir peleando
esa muerte no me apena,
no me apena morir dando
sangre que vive en mis venas

Granada, cómo te hieren
los marines que te arrancan
la lengua y la cabellera
para devorar tu alma.

Granada, tu fosa es mía
como es mía la sementera
sobre el arrecife pardo
donde anidaron las hienas.

Quiero morir frente al mar,
con mi fusil encarnado
y un ruiseñor instalando
su canto nunca acabado.

Cuaderno de Granada

THE NIGHTINGALE AND DEATH

If I am going to die fighting
that death does not sadden me,
it does not sadden me to die spilling
blood which lives in my veins.

Grenada, how the marines
wound you who pull out
your tongue and your hair
in order to devour your soul.

Grenada, your grave is mine
as is mine the planted field
on the dun coral
where the hyenas have their lair.

I want to die by the sea,
with my gun bloodied
and a nightingale starting up
his never-ending song.

Grenada Notebook

GRANADINA

Soy granadina.
Sembré nueces moscadas
bajo el amparo fijo
del flamboyán silvestre
y volví a echar las redes
en el azul de los veranos.
Hierbas, rocas y conchas
acunaron el corazón de mis aldeas
y el cielo fue testigo
de cómo hambreaban por el puerto
todos mis hijos.

Soy granadina.
Vi los humos, de pronto,
vivos ahora entre los muertos,
entre la furia y el relámpago.
He descubierto el esencial mañana
nuentras cavo la tumba de un marine
que osó cavar la mía tras el acecho impune
a una muchacha de Saint-George.
Soy granadina
y aquí yaces, tendido,
esperando el responso de las serpientes.

Cuaderno de Granada

GRENADIAN WOMAN

I am a Grenadian woman.
I sowed nutmegs
beneath the fixed shelter
of the wild flamboyant tree
and I cast the nets again
into the blue of the summers.
Grasses, rocks and conch shells
cradled the heart of my villages
and the sky was witness
to how all my sons
hungered around the port.

I am a Grenadian woman.
I saw the smoke, suddenly,
alive now among the dead,
between the fury and the lightning.
I have discovered the essential morning
while I dig the grave of a marine
who dared to dig mine after stalking unpunished
a girl from Saint George.
I am a Grenadian woman
and here you lie, stretched out,
waiting for the response of the serpents.

Grenada Notebook

ELEGÍA A MAURICE BISHOP

"Nadie lo podrá matar"
Nicolás Guillén

El cuervo grazna
enloquecido
revoloteando
allá en lo alto.
Dos torvos nubarrones
van descendiendo
hasta la roca fría.
Silban el viento y la lechuza
sobre una isla.
Hay una voz de muerte
renacida.Y el mar,
el mar antiguo de las sales,
del arpón y las ninfas,
bate sus olas seculares
y se deshace en las palmeras.
Hay una voz de muerte impía.

Toco la frente de este muerto
y nadie me responde.
¿En qué ola se ha disuelto su sangre?
¿En qué galeón hundido,
en cuál golpe del viento?
Toco a todas las puertas de Saint-George
y nadie sabe responderme.
¿En qué nube del trópico
late el recuerdo de este hombre?

ELEGY FOR MAURICE BISHOP

> *"Nobody will be able to kill him"*
> Nicolás Guillén

The crow caws
maddened
flying around
up in the sky.
Two baleful big clouds
are coming down
to the cold rock.
The wind and the owl whistle
over an island.
There is a voice of death
reborn. And the sea,
the ancient sea of salt,
of the harpoon and the nymphs,
beats its secular waves
and undoes itself in the palm trees.
There is a voice of death impious.

I knock on the forehead of this dead man
and nobody answers me.
In which wave has his blood dissolved itself?
In which sunken galleon,
in which gust of wind?
I knock on all the doors of Saint George
and nobody is able to answer me.
In which cloud of the tropic
beats the memory of this man?

Saint-George flota en silencio
como si conociera el crimen de antemano.
Toqué los ojos de los pescadores.
Nadie supo decirme.
Toqué a la puerta de una iglesia
acribillada y vacia.
Toqué los labios de una siempreviva
y adiviné el misterio.
El muerto no está muerto.
El muerto ruge en la sabana.
El muerto alienta en las salinas,
va en andas entre el pueblo
que lo planta sobre el arca de las colinas
y lo arma de un lenguaje afiebrado.
Saint-George gime en silencio
como un niño.

Toqué la punta de las bayonetas
y nadie sospechaba.
Toqué la sangre fúlgida de los caídos
cuando nadie me viera.
Con mi pequeña daga,
abrí el lomo de los anfibios verdes
y la traición reinaba.
Toqué el rostro siniestro de los guardias
y ninguno veía.
Toqué el corazón del muerto
dormido entre las hierbas
como un baobab recién talado.
Su boca indicaba el camino
hacia la manigua inmensa
donde el pasado jamás fue libre o bueno
o verdaderamente pasado.

Saint Georges floats in silence
as if it knew about the crime already.
I knocked on the eyes of the fishermen.
Nobody was able to tell me.
I knocked on the door of a church
bullet-riddled and empty.
I knocked on the lips of an immortelle
and divined the mystery.
The dead man is not dead.
The dead man roars in the sheet.
The dead man breathes in the salt marshes,
he is carried shoulder-high among the people
who place him on the ark of the hills
and arm him with a fevered language.
Saint Georges moans in silence,
like a child.

I touched the points of the bayonets
and nobody suspected.
I touched the resplendent blood of the fallen
when nobody might see me.
With my small dagger,
I opened the backs of the green amphibians
and treason reigned.
I touched the sinister faces of the guards
and none saw.
I touched the heart of the dead man
asleep in the grasses
like a recently-felled baobab.
His mouth pointed the way
towards the immense swamp
where the past was never free nor good
or truly the past.

Ocho cabezas furtivas,
ocho cabezas de amianto,
van escoltando su marcha entre las ramas.
Ocho pechos de viejos cimarrones en una larga travesía.
El Olonés bogando y blasfemando entre la niebla
y el espectro de Dessalines aullando:
–¡Maurice! ¡Maurice!
El hacha del verdugo brilla en tus ojos como nunca.

Ni los marines, ni el Pentágono,
ni los banqueros de Manhattan,
ni los despachos de la prensa,
ni los rockets del dólar,
ni los gobernadores de palo,
ni los mensajes diplomáticos,
ni las argucias de la CIA
impiden que este muerto
acuda con afán a sus deberes y a su cita.
Los constructores lo acompañan.

El muerto no está muerto
sino que habla junto al limo y junto al arrecife
a las islas del Sur.
Ay, Mar Caribe, he visto
sangre de negro bullendo en las calderas,
sangre emanando de sus pulmones negros
y las prisiones abarrotándose de lágrimas
y los cerros en pie sus puños levantando.
Otra vez sangre y sangre derramada.
Un alcatraz pasa volando.
¡Qué llanto y qué soledad,
qué soledad y qué llanto!

Cuadernos de Granada

Eight furtive heads,
eight asbestos heads,
are escorting his progress between the branches.
Eight chests of old runaway slaves in a long passage.
El Olonés rowing and cursing in the fog
and the spectre of Dessalines howling:
– Maurice! Maurice!
The hangman's axe shines in your eyes as never before.

Neither the marines, nor the Pentagon,
nor the Manhattan bankers,
nor the press dispatches,
nor the dollar rockets,
nor the puppet governors,
nor the diplomatic messages,
nor the cunning of the CIA
will prevent this dead man
attending with eagerness to his duties and his appointment.
The builders accompany him.

The dead man is not dead
rather he speaks beside the lime tree and beside the coral
to the islands of the South.
Ay, Caribbean Sea, I have seen
the blood of blacks bubbling in the cauldrons,
blood emanating from their black lungs
and the prisons packing themselves with tears
and the hills standing up raising their fists.
Once more blood and spilt blood.
An albatross flies by.
What lament and what aloneness,
what aloneness and what lament!

Grenada Notebook

HISTORIA

Apenas vengo del cerco,
apenas puedo llorar,
el obús llega planeando
sobre el mar

Apenas vengo del cerro,
apenas puedo llorar,
mis dedos, la mejor arma
frente al mar.

Apenas vengo del huerto,
apenas puedo llorar,
apenas nace Granada
donde el mar.

Cuaderno de Granada

HISTORY

I have hardly come from the siege,
I can hardly cry,
the mortar arrives soaring
over the sea.

I have hardly come from the hills,
I can hardly cry,
my fingers, the best weapon
facing the sea.

I have hardly come from the market garden,
I can hardly cry,
Grenada is hardly born
by the sea.

Grenada Notebook

Junto al Golfo

"galeotes dramáticos, galeotes dramáticos"
Nicolás Guillén

La meseta del indio
nos avisa
la fragancia del golfo.
Manatí,
         flecha en boca,
atrapa el archipiélago de su jardín.
Orillas enlutadas,
dientes de tiburón,
las gubias y las conchas,
los valles olorosos,
transparencias del cielo a la corriente,
entre las firmes playas del golfo:

Islas sobre islas. Islas del canto.
Islas. Canto del mar sobre las Islas.
Y mis ojos que bogan
por los bordes humeantes de las hierbas.

Caribe de la asfixia, tu pasado perdido,
tu habla y tu pulmón.
El verde de la flecha,
las ciudades perpetuas de la Luna,
los calendarios,
las humaredas
pero veo
         "los galeotes dramáticos,"

BY THE GULF

> *"dramatic galleons, dramatic galleons"*
> Nicolás Guillén

The plateau of the Indian
alerts us
to the fragrance of the gulf.
Manatee,
                    arrow in mouth,
traps the archipelago from its garden.
Shores in mourning,
sharks' teeth,
the stone chips and the conch shells,
the sweet-smelling valleys,
transparencies of the sky on the current,
among the firm beaches of the gulf:

Islands on islands. Islands of song.
Islands. The song of the sea on the Islands.
And my eyes which row
along the steamy borders of the grasses.

Caribbean of asphyxia, your lost past,
your speech and your lungs.
The green of the arrow,
the perpetual cities of the Moon,
the calendars,
the clouds of smoke
but I see
            "the dramatic galleons",

el corsario sombrío
con su arco de napalm
en el fondo del golfo.

Cimarrón en la noche estamos en las aguas
azules y encuentras nuevas islas
nuevos seres
                    que nadan junto al mar.
La brisa en el atardecer de cobre,
el sol naciente
sobre la espalda de mil años,
vibración del lagarto,
puente de las bodegas,
el rayo de Changó y el chivo.

La sangre es quien nos pide
la urgencia
                    de este mundo:
Alzad las lanzas,
                    las retinas,
la miel y el garabato
que somos el golfo para siempre.

Octubre imprescindible

the sombre corsair
with its arch of napalm
in the depths of the gulf.

A runaway slave in the night we are in the blue
waters and you find new islands
new beings
            who swim beside the sea.
The breeze in the copper sunset,
the dawning sun
on the back of a thousand years,
vibration of the lizard,
bridge of the hold,
the ray of Changó and the goat.

Blood is what asks us
for the urgency
            of this world:
Raise the lances,
            the retinas,
the honey and the hook
for we are the gulf for ever.

Indispensable October

Historia de un Pastor

Qué tristes son las cosas que han pasado.
Mataron al cordero y a la cabra.
Mataron a los hijos del cazador
y saquearon sus chozas.
Nada pudo quedar en pie
sino la lluvia fina
sobre la tierra calcinada
y el plumaje cenizo de un ruiseñor.
El humo iba elevándose
desde el estiércol
de las ovejas.
En medio de la colina gris,
hay un pastor sin lágrimas
con su túnica blanca.
Tiene el rostro apacible
y, mientras pasea su mirada
a través del paisaje
allá en lo alto de la colina,
aparta tierra húmeda
y siembra unas semillas elementales,
con sus manos tranquilas.

Un ave cruza el cielo.
La boca del pastor entona, a solas,
una plegaria también elemental
que termina con estas palabras:
África estás en mí.
Aquí planto una brizna de aliento,
aquí renaceremos.

THE STORY OF A SHEPHERD

How sad are the things that have happened.
They killed the lamb and the goat.
They killed the children of the hunter
and ransacked their huts.
Nothing could remain standing
except the fine rain
on the burnt land
and the ashen plumage of a nightingale.
The smoke was rising up
from the manure
of the sheep.
In the middle of the grey hill,
there is a shepherd without tears,
with his white tunic.
He has a peaceful face
and, while he moves his gaze
across the landscape
there on the high part of the hill,
he opens humid earth
and sows elemental seeds
with his tranquil hands.

A bird crosses the sky.
The mouth of the shepherd utters, alone,
a prayer also elemental
which ends in these words:
"Africa you are in me.
Here I plant a drizzle of breath,
here we will be reborn.

Aquí seremos dueños otra vez
de nuestros días y nuestros bosques.
Volveremos al país eterno de nuestros padres,
al país de nuestros sueños.

Baladas para un sueño

Here we will be owners once again
of our days and our woods.
We will return to the eternal country of our fathers,
to the country of our dreams."

Ballads for a Dream

BAAS

Eres el amo.
Azares y un golpe seco de la historia
te hicieron ser mi amo.
Tienes la tierra toda
y yo tengo la pena.
Tienes la hacienda,
el potro, el olivo, los rifles
y yo tengo la pena.
En medio de la noche
te alzas como una bestia en celo.
Tuyos mi sudor y mis manos.
Me has hecho nómada en mis propios confines.
Eres el amo
y eres esclavo
de lo que posees.
Eres el amo.
Me has despojado de mis cosas
pero no de mi canto.
¿Qué vas a hacer
cuando me alce mañana
y recobre mi potro, mi olivo
y mis estrellas.

Baladas para un sueño

Baas

You are the master.
Luck and a sudden coup of history
made you my master.
You have all the land
and I have the suffering.
You have the ranch,
the colt, the olive tree, the rifles
and I have the suffering.
In the middle of the night
you rise up like a beast in heat.
Yours my sweat and my hands.
You have made me a nomad in my own territory.
You are the master
and you are a slave
to what you possess.
You are the master.
You have stripped me of my things
but not of my song.
What are you going to do
when I rise up tomorrow
and take back my colt, my olive tree
and my stars?

Ballads for a Dream

Soliloquio de un Colono

Acabo de degollar a un ovambo.
¿Qué es un ovambo?
Un negro,
un animal rabioso,
un monstruo con apenas dos patas
y dos ojos inmensos como de Lucifer.
Eran como las seis de la tarde
y los dos tropezamos,
saliendo de la granja,
frente al jardín de la señora Woolf.
Las adelfas de la señora Woolf son tan hermosas.
Yo se las riego los domingos cuando sale de compras
                                        a Pretoria.
Dije que tropezó conmigo y no se disculpó.
Alzó la cabeza y no se disculpó.
Era un grosero, como todos los negros,
un ovambo de los infiernos,
un terrorista, un depredador,
un negro ovambo,
y no me pude contener
y fui a buscar la soga y la navaja.
Ya estaba a espaldas cuado lo derribé...
Eso fue todo, Peter.
Yo bien respeto el orden y la ley.
¿Jugamos a las cartas?

Baladas para un sueño

SOLILOQUY OF A COLONIAL

I've just cut the throat of an ovambo.
What's an ovambo?
A kaffir
a rabid animal
a monster with only two paws
and two immense eyes like Lucifer.
It was around six in the evening
and we bumped into each other
coming out of the farm
across from Mrs Woolf's garden.
Mrs Woolf's oleanders are so beautiful.
I water them for her on Sundays when she goes
                                    shopping to Pretoria.
I said he bumped into me and did not beg my pardon.
He raised his head and did not beg my pardon.
He had no manners, like all the kaffirs,
an ovambo from hell,
a terrorist, a looter,
a kaffir ovambo,
and I couldn't contain myself
and I went to get the noose and the knife.
He had already turned his back when I brought him
                                    down...

That was all, Peter.
I'm all for law and order.
Shall we play cards?

Ballads for a Dream

ANIVERSARIO

Ya había cortado diez rosas para Vinnia
cuando atravesé el bantustán
casi dormido
al vaivén del trino
de los gallos.
Era nuestro primer aniversario.
Me detuvieron.
Me preguntaron.
Y entregué el pase.
La blanca luz de la mañana
crecía y crecía
inundando el mercado.
Caminé sin aliento
hasta llegar a la ciudad.
Un comericante corre detrás de una sirvienta
ofreciéndole un dólar estrujado.
Era nuestro primer aniversario.
Me detuvieron.
Me preguntaron.
Y entregué el pase.
Los autmóviles bajaban.
Las rastras ascendían.
Mi corazón se desbordaba
a lo largo de la avenida.
El sol, más fuerte aún,
como una yema congelada.
Me detuvieron.
Me preguntaron.
Y entregué el pase.

ANNIVERSARY

I had already cut ten roses for Vinnia
when I crossed the Bantustan
half-asleep
to the coming and going of the crowing
of the cocks.
It was our first anniversary.
I was stopped.
I was questioned.
And I handed over my pass.
The white light of the morning
grew and grew
inundating the market.
I walked breathless
until I arrived at the city.
A shopkeeper runs after a maid
offering her a scrunched-up dollar.
It was our first anniversary.
I was stopped.
I was questioned.
And I handed over my pass.
The cars were going down.
The harrows were going up.
My heart was overflowing
all along the avenue.
The sun, stronger still,
like a frozen egg-yolk.
I was stopped.
I was questioned.
And I handed over my pass.

Llegué al bantustán de Vinnia
pasadas las seis de la tarde.
La busqué con la vista
y con ansias de amor.
Vinnia, ¿has dudado de mí?
Salí temprano se mi bantustán
pero me detuvieron,
me preguntaron
y entregué el pase.
Anduve un laberinto para llegar aquí,
le dije, con la cabeza gacha,
como un ladrón a quien sorprenden.
Su rostro era una mezcla
de aflicción y impaciencia.

Tan bella Vinnia frente a su bantustán
pero mis rosas estaban ya marchitas.
Era nuestro primer aniversario.

Baladas para un sueño

I arrived at Vinnia's Bantustan
after six o'clock in the evening.
I looked for her with my eyes
and with the anxieties of love.
Vinnia did you doubt me?
I left my Bantustan early
but I was stopped,
I was questioned
and I handed over my pass.
I walked through a labyrinth to get here,
I told her, with my head down,
like a thief caught in the act.
Her face was a mixture
of affliction and impatience.

Vinnia so lovely in her Bantustan
but my roses were already withered.
It was our first anniversary.

Ballads for a Dream

Ritornello

Winnie Mandela
¿dónde estás?
Winnie Mandela
¿cuándo vienes?
Winnie Mandela
donde estés
te esperan los sinsontes
y las alamedas
Winnie Mandela
¿dónde estás?
Winnie Mandela
¿cuándo vienes?
Winnie Mandela
¿vuelves del cabo
o del Transkei,
Winnie Mandela?
Winnie Mandela
¿dónde estás?
Winnie Mandela
¿cuándo vuelves?
Winnie Mandela
te esperamos
Winnie Mandela
libre y fuerte.

Baladas para un sueño

RITORNELLO

Winnie Mandela
where are you?
Winnie Mandela
when are you coming?
Winnie Mandela
wherever you are
the mocking-birds are waiting for you
and the poplar trees
Winnie Mandela
where are you?
Winnie Mandela
when are you coming?
Winnie Mandela
are you coming back from the Cape
or the Transkei,
Winnie Mandela?
Winnie Mandela
where are you?
Winnie Mandela
when are you coming back?
Winnie Mandela
we are waiting for you
Winnie Mandela
free and strong.

Ballads for a Dream

COCINERA

A las cinco llega a la granja.
"Buenos días mi amo",
suele decir sin ganas
como una ley vigente del demonio.
Cocina, da de comer al dueño
y al papagayo;
lava los platos, los ordena
y sale a comer en una lata
junto al corral del patio.
Una hora después,
recoge a los perros del amo
y les sirve su plato favorito
en la sala de mármol del comedor lustroso.

Baladas para un sueño

COOK

At five she arrives at the farm.
"Good morning, baas",
she usually says unwillingly
as if it were a law enforced by the Devil.
She cooks, she feeds her employer
and the parrot;
washes the dishes, puts them away
and goes out to eat out of a tin
next to the animal pen in the farmyard.
An hour later,
she takes the boss's dogs
and gives them their favourite food
on the marble furniture of the shining dining-room.

Ballads for a Dream

Balada de la Cárcel de Robben

*"Ser libre es una cosa que sólo un hombre sabe: sólo el hombre
que advierte dentro una mazmorra como su ya estuviera"*
Miguel Hernández

Los pajarillos hacen dormir los sueños de Mandela
que había olvidado el sabor del salitre,
la frescura del cielo, los resplandores del desierto.
Una sombra gigante se apoderó de las montañas,
del sobrio suelo del Transkei
y lanzó un aullido violento de alimaña.
Desde entonces un preso inmemorial
canta a los ocres de la isla
desde su celda...
En un verano abrasador,
sus manos se aliviaron con el oasis
que le traía su amada.
Lo habían cercado tanto
que no escuchaba el viento de los arrecifes,
ni el rumoroso aliento de las hierbas,
ni veía el sol,
ni el aro de la luna brillando en las alturas.
Lo confinaron a soledades firmes
y han hecho lo indecible por cortarle la lengua,
por atarle los pies y las manos
hasta podarle el corazón.
Mandela, junto al cantar de olas y aves,
abrió los surcos en la tierra
y los regó con agua de su boca.
Sin salir de su celda,

The Ballad of Robben Island Gaol

"Being free is something only a man knows: only the man
who behaves inside a dungeon as if he already were free".
Miguel Hernández

The little birds put to sleep the dreams of Mandela
who had forgotten the taste of saltpetre,
the freshness of the sky, the splendours of the desert.
A giant shadow took over the mountains,
the sober land of the Transkei
and let out the violent howl of a carrion beast.
Since then an immemorial prisoner
sings to the ochres of the island
from his cell...
In a burning summer
his hands found relief in the oasis
his beloved would bring him.
They had enclosed him so much
that he could not hear the wind on the reefs,
nor the murmuring breath of the grasses,
nor could he see the sun,
nor the ring of the moon shining on high.
They kept him in solitary confinement
and they did the unspeakable to cut out his tongue,
to tie his feet and hands
even to pollard his heart.
Mandela, next to the song of waves and birds,
opened furrows in the earth
and irrigated them with the water of his mouth.
Without leaving his cell,

todo lo ve, todo lo toca,
todo lo vuelve flecha contra el hierro candente
de sus amargos carceleros.
Desde un ricón inusitado
va lanzando su flor de amores patrios
por las praderas de Namibia,
sobre las costas de la Ciudad del Cabo,
sobre el asfalto ensangrentado de Johannesburgo,
entre los cuerpos de los imbondeiros angolanos,
sobre Guinea y el Congo,
sobre Nubia y Cartago,
sobre los archipiélagos del Índico
y las imensas aguas del Nilo.
Mandela voló sobre su celda
para cantar esta balada
de la cárcel de Robben.

Baladas para un sueño

he sees everything, he touches everything,
he turns everything into an arrow against the red-
                                            hot steel
of his bitter gaolers.
From a little-known corner
he continues to throw out his flower of love of
                                            country
through the meadows of Namibia,
over the coasts of Cape Town,
over the bloodied asphalt of Johannesburg,
among the bodies of the Angolan bond-rebels,
over Guinea and the Congo,
over Nubia and Carthage,
over the archipelagos of the Indian Ocean
and the immense waters of the Nile.
Mandela flew over his cell
to sing this ballad
of Robben Island gaol.

Ballads for a Dream

Epitafio para una Dama De Pretoria

Sobre una idea del poeta Countee Cullen

Siempre pensó que aún resurrecta
dormiría la mañana
hasta que tres ángeles negros
le hicieran bien la cama
y, sobre todo, el desayuno.

Baladas para un sueño

EPITAPH FOR A PRETORIA LADY

From an idea by the Poet Countee Cullen

She always thought that even when resurrected
she would sleep in the morning
until three black angels
made her bed properly
and, above all, her breakfast.

Ballads for a Dream

Nana Silente para Niños Surafricanos

Mamá no tenía pase
y no había pan.
Papá no tenía pase
        y lo habían castigado.
Mamá no tenía pase
y no había pan.
Papá no tenía pase
        y murió degollado.
Mamá no tenía pase
y no había pan.

Baladas para un sueño

SILENT LULLABY FOR SOUTH AFRICAN CHILDREN

Mamma didn't have a pass
and there was no bread.
Papa didn't have a pass
      and they had punished him.
Mamma didn't have a pass
and there was no bread.
Papa didn't have a pass
      and he died with his throat slit.
Mamma didn't have a pass
and there was no bread.

Ballads for a Dream

II

Paisaje Célebre

Ver la caída de Ícaro desde la bahía de
azules y verdes de Alamar.

Un valle al que se asoma
un misántropo encapuchado.
Árboles frutales alrededor de las aguas
y un hombrecillo, solo, arando sobre ellas
hasta incorporarse al arcoiris.

Ese hombrecillo
es un pariente de Brueghel, el viejo, hermano mío,
que pinta la soledad del alma
cercada por espléndidos labradores.

Es el atardecer y necesito las alas de Ícaro.

Paisaje célebre

Famous Landscape

To see the fall of Icarus from the bay of
blues and greens of Alamar.

A valley into which stoops
a hooded misanthrope.
Fruit trees around the waters
and a little man, alone, ploughing around them
until he blends into the rainbow.

That little man
is a relative of Brueghel, the elder, brother of mine,
who paints the aloneness of the soul
surrounded by splendid labourers.

It is dusk and I need the wings of Icarus.

Famous Landscape

Ante un Espejo

A Sonia Rivera Valdés

Si decidieras irte de la ciudad,
de tu ciudad,
en busca de nuevos horizontes,
de fortuna
o tal vez de una pasión sin precedentes,
la ciudad, esta ciudad,
aún inconciente de sus ruinas,
emprenderá tu acecho
siguiéndote los pasos.
Alguna tarde cálida
(tú sobre los puentes
de algún río caudaloso pero ajeno)
nuestra ciudad sepultará,
bajo un aroma extraño,
los años transcurridos
antes y después de Cristo.
No hay otro país, ni otra ciudad posibles.
Cuando haya amanecer, no habrá crepúsculo.
Si los parques florecen
cundidos de tulipanes firmes,
entonces el bulevar trae los olores
de tus seres queridos
y, sobre todo, de tus muertos.
Si decidieras irte,
el puerto y las bahías
y los Jardines de la Reina
te escoltarán con sus vapores.

In Front of a Mirror

To Sonia Rivera Valdés

If you were to decide to go away from the city,
from your city,
in search of new horizons,
of fortune
or perhaps a passion without precedents,
the city, this city,
still unconscious of its ruins,
would undertake to stalk you
following your footsteps.
Some warm evening
(you on a bridge
of some voluminous but alien river)
our city would entomb,
under a strange aroma,
the years which have passed
before and after Christ.
There is no other possible country, nor another city.
When it would be dawn, there would be no dusk.
If the parks bloom
smothered with firm tulips,
then the boulevard will bring the smells
of your beloved beings
and, above all, of your dead.
If you were to decide to go,
the port and the bays
and the Queen's Gardens
would escort you with their vapours.

Recorrerás los mismos pasadizos,
los barrios arcaicos del estruendo
con la indolencia de sus bares;
no valdrá un solo verso de Blaise Cendrars
y hasta los mismos cuartos de tu casa sellada
te cercarán con la angustiosa cadencia del engaño.
A donde quiera que te muevas
escucharás el mismo pregón de la mañana;
te llevará el mismo barco andando por la misma ruta
de los perennes emigrantes.
Nada podrá depositarte en ningún sitio.
Aunque hayas monteado el mundo entero,
de castillo en castillo,
de mercado en mercado,
ésta será la ciudad de todos tus fantasmas.
Habrás desgastado tu vida un poco inútilmente
y cuando ya estés vieja,
ante un espejo como el de Cenicienta
sonreirás algo triste
y en tus pupilas secas
habrá dos rocas fieles
y una esquina sonora de tu ciudad.

Paisaje célebre

You would pass through the same passageways,
the old bustling quarters
with the indolence of their bars;
not a single verse of Blaise Centrars would be worth
                                                anything
and even the very rooms of your sealed house
would lay siege to you with the anguished cadence
                                                of deception.
Wherever you were to go
you would hear the same cry of the morning;
the same boat would take you along the same route
of the perennial emigrants.
Nothing would be able to set you down anywhere.
Even if you were to have hunted the whole world over,
from castle to castle,
from market to market,
this would be the city of all your ghosts.
You would have spent all your life a little uselessly
and then when you were old,
in front of a mirror like that of Cinderella
you would smile somewhat sad
and in the dry pupils of your eyes
there would be two loyal rocks
and a sonorous corner of your city.

                    Famous Landscape

Mujer con Pescado

A la memoria de Luis Martínez Pedro

A la vista, una mujer oscura
que se avecina
con un solo pescado.
Lo trae prisionero en el puño
como para evitar que se le escape del horno
el último de los mohicanos.
A simple vista, sus cinco dedos
son una jaula grande para el pescado
quien, con un ojo alerta, va cabeceando
y aleteando y soñando con chorros de algas vivas
y largos delfines y nelumbios
desde un fondo azul marino con muelle milenario
por donde transitar
hasta que el cándido pero implacable anzuelo
lo reconozca y lo intercepte
en medio del camino hacia las orillas de Cayo Hueso
sobre cuya arena languidece una puesta de sol
y un óleo con palmeras de Gregorio Valdés.

Paisaje célebre

WOMAN WITH FISH

To the memory of Luis Martínez Pedro

In view, a dark woman
who is drawing near
with a single fish.
She is carrying it prisoner in her fist
as if to avoid its escaping the oven on her
the last of the Mohicans.
In plain view, her five fingers
are a big cage for the fish
which, with an alert eye, is shaking its head
and flapping and dreaming of streams of live algae
and long dolphins and nelumbos
in a navy blue background with a millenarian dock
through which to pass
until the candid but implacable hook
recognises it and intercepts it
in the middle of the journey to the shores of Key West
on whose beach a sunset languishes
and an oil painting with palm trees by Gregorio Valdés.

Famous Landscape

MARINA

Frente a los barcos
fondeados,
hay una cartomántica
que espera la opción cero
y pone su pamela
sobre el muro del malecón.
Pasa un coche tirado
por un caballo flaco
frente a los barcos
fondeados.
La cartomántica vuelve la cabeza
y ve los ojos del caballo flaco
sin jinete y sin rumbo,
frente a los barcos
fondeados.
Hay un caballo flaco
y una mujer que aguarda
la caída de la tarde,
sin una dalia entre las manos,
frente a los barcos
fondeados.

Paisaje célebre

MARINA

In front of the anchored
boats,
there is a fortune teller
who waits for the zero option
and puts her straw hat
on the wall of the jetty.
A car pulled
by a thin horse
passes in front of the anchored
boats.
The fortune teller turns her head
and looks into the eyes of the thin horse
riderless and directionless,
in front of the anchored
boats.
There is a thin horse
and a woman who waits
for the fall of evening,
without a dahlia in her hands
in front of the anchored
boats.

Famous Landscape

Dibujo

En las afueras de la ciudad,
hay un camino estrecho y polvoriento;
seco, extrañamente seco y, por ello mismo,
el polvo
es más fosforescente:
        un polvo seco
que se adentra en los humores del cuerpo.
Una jungla adversa aparece;
el poeta la divisa o, mejor dicho, quiero decir,
divisa
a la negrita escuálida que se agarra al tubo de la ruta 7
como queriendo resistir todos los embates de este
        momento;
resistiendo a los golpes mortales sin más ni más.
Yo hablaba de una jungla adversa y me faltó decir
que es verde, de un verde botella, de un verde mar,
de un verde acqua, de un verde cauce,
        monte de cristal verde ahumándose.
Aún así, San Francisco de Paula, has entrado en mi
        corazón.
Tu rara presencia y tu follaje intenso de invernadero
me recuerdan la aspiración precisa de Ernest
        Hemingway
quien tal vez vio en tu fronda un remedo interior
de los bosques de Michigan.

DRAWING

On the outskirts of the city,
there is a narrow and dusty road;
dry, extremely dry and, because of that,
the dust
is more phosphorescent:
        a dry dust
which gets into the humours of the body.
An adverse jungle appears;
the poet makes it out, or rather, I mean to say,
makes out
the squalid little black woman who hangs onto the
        rail on route 7
as if she wished to resist all the batterings of this
        moment;
resisting the mortal blows nothing more nor less.
I was speaking of an adverse jungle and I should have
        said
that it is green, a bottle green, a sea green,
an aqua green, a river-channel green,
        a mountain of green glass smoking itself.
Even so, San Francisco de Paula, you have got into
        my heart.
Your rare presence and your intense greenhouse
        foliage
remind me of the precise aspiration of Ernest
        Hemingway
who perhaps saw in your fronds a poor internal
        imitation
of the woods of Michigan.

"¿Cómo serán los bosques de Michigan?",
se pregunta la escuálida negrita
que se desplaza para tomar un asiento libre,
el único asiento libre de todo el mediodía.
La pregunta es ociosa porque los verdes
de San Francisco de Paula los sustituyen
y los vencen en su manifiesto fulgor,
manifiesto.
        El asunto es
que este es un dibujo, casi un daguerrotipo.
El universo de Hemingway y el de la negrita son
                      diferentes
pero han transcurrido en un mismo escenario terrestre
donde lo que cuenta
es el deseo de vivir
de vivir
a pesar
de

Paisaje célebre

"What are the Michigan woods like?",
the squalid little black woman who moves
to take up a free seat asks herself,
the only free seat of the whole midday.
The question is idle because the greens
of San Francisco de Paula take their place
and defeat them in their manifest brilliance,
manifest.
                    The point is
that this is a drawing, almost a daguerrotype.
The universe of Hemingway and that of the little
                          black woman are different
but they have taken place in the same terrestrial
                                      scenario
in which what counts
is the desire to live
to live
in spite
of

Famous Landscape

Piedra Pulida

Un nuevo libro,
un nuevo día,
otra nueva ciudad,
más veranos, más flores,
aquel perpetuo mar
y yo, ahora,
sobre piedra pulida,
busco tus labios,
busco tus ojos.

Piedra pulida

POLISHED STONE

A new book,
a new day,
another new city,
more summers, more flowers,
that perpetual sea
and I, now,
on polished stone,
search for your lips.
search for your eyes.

Polished Stone

ORÉGANO

En el naufragio de las barcazas
perdí el olor del orégano
que estaba sembrado
en un ingenio antiguo de la Marie-Galante.
Vino el pirata
y se llevó su aroma
de tierra y planta buena.
Vendrán los hierros
de las algas marinas
para avivar de nuevo su raíz
inscrita en la roca musgosa
de un sueño milenario.

Paisaje célebre

OREGANO

In the shipwreck of the lighters
I lost the smell of the oregano
which was sown
in an old sugar-mill of the Marie-Galante.
The pirate came
and took away with him its aroma
of earth and herbs.
The iron of the marine algae
will come
to liven up its root again
inscribed on the mossy rock
of a millennial sleep.

Famous Landscape

Botella al Mar

A Mario Benedetti y Luz

Una botella de vino tinto al mar.
Son las tres de la tarde.
Una botella de vino tinto sin licor,
sin apenas los restos de esos vapores
que nos transportan a lo indecible.
Una botella con un mensaje
¿para quién?
Era un papel muy blanco
emborronado con una escritura
minúscula casi ilegible. Allí decía:
"Escribo en este papel
que introduzco en esta botella
para Nadie
y para todo aquel
o aquella
que quisiera leerme
en las próximas eras."
Salta un pez desde la espuma
y tumba el lápiz y el papel
con los cuales me expreso.
Ruedan los dos
y sobre el mar
de grafito
viene un galeón diminuto
y unos negros
amordazados
dando alaridos

BOTTLE IN THE SEA

To Mario Benedetti y Luz

A red-wine bottle in the sea.
It's three in the afternoon.
A red-wine bottle with no liquor in it,
with hardly any remains of those vapours
which transport us to the unsayable.
A bottle with a message
for whom?
It was a very white piece of paper
smudged with a minuscule
almost illegible handwriting. There it said:
"I'm writing on this piece of paper
which I'm putting into this bottle
for Nobody
and for all those men
or women
who may wish to read me
in times to come."
A fish jumps out of the foam
and the pencil and the paper
with which I'm expressing myself fall.
Both roll
and on the sea
of graffiti
a diminutive galleon comes
and blacks
gagged
howling

y una niña hermosa y sola
de pupilas abiertas
y un duendecillo feo pero audaz.
Había escrito estas peripecias
con el aliento del salitre
cuando el papel regresó a mis manos
como por arte de magia...
"A quien pueda interesar:
buenos días, buenas noches".
Una botella de vino tinto al mar.
Son las tres de la tarde.

Paisaje célebre

and a beautiful girl on her own
the pupils of her eyes open
and an ugly but audacious little spirit.
I had written these incidents
with the breath of the salt residue
when the paper returned to my hands
as if by magical art...
"To whom it may concern:
Good Day, Good Night".
A red-wine bottle in the sea.
It's three in the afternoon.

Famous Landscape

Intuición

¿Cómo es que puedo atravesar el viento
y preguntarme si este viento
es esa libertad cuyo nombre apuntamos
en la libreta infantil
que hoy he descubierto
como un paisaje lunar, iluminado por sombras
polares, hecho para otros ojos
que no son los míos?

Paisaje célebre

INTUITION

How is it I can cross the wind
and ask myself if this wind
is that liberty whose name we jot down
in the childish copybook
which today I have discovered
like a lunar landscape, illuminated by polar
shadows, made for other eyes
which are not mine?

Famous Landscape

El Tambor

Mi cuerpo convoca la llama.

Mi cuerpo convoca los humos.

Mi cuerpo en el desastre
como un pájaro blando.

Mi cuerpo como islas.

Mi cuerpo junto a las catedrales.

Mi cuerpo en el coral.

Aires los de mi bruma.

Fuego sobre mis aguas.

Aguas irreversibles
en los azules de la tierra.

Mi cuerpo en plenilunio.

Mi cuerpo como las codornices.

Mi cuerpo en una pluma.

Mi cuerpo al sacrificio.

Mi cuerpo en la penumbra.

TAMBOR

My body summons flame.

My body summons smoke.

My body in disaster
like a soft bird.

My body like islands.

My body next to the cathedrals.

My body in the coral.

Airs, those of my fog.

Fire over my waters.

Irreversible waters
in the blues of the land.

My body at full moon.

My body like quails.

My body in a feather.

My body to the sacrifice.

My body in penumbra.

Mi cuerpo en claridad.
Mi cuerpo ingrávido en la luz
vuestra, libre, en el arco.

Elogio de la danza

My body in clarity.
My weightless body in your
light, free, in the arc.

Eulogy of the Dance

III

Mirar Adentro

Del siglo dieciseis data mi pena
y apenas lo sabía
porque aquel ruiseñor
siempre canta en mi pena.

Piedra pulida

LOOKING INWARDS

From the sixteenth century my suffering dates
and I hardly knew it
because that nightingale
always sings in my suffering.

Polished Stone

Humus Inmemorial

En Jovellanos, la flor de Jericó.
Madre que hallas tu vientre
por entre grillos y ramales,
esta es tu playa.

El cielo blanco surcado por los rayos.
El mar grisáceo de las bodegas
sacando a borbotones
negros amordazados,
echándolos,
entre la bruma,
sobre un puerto cualquiera.

Moza, madre que hallas tu vientre
por entre fieras y osamentas,
mira al guardiero,
celador de tus pasos,
consumirse,
cercado y preso.

Bestia de carga fuimos.

En la llanura de Jovellanos,
la flor de Jericó.
Oh la llanura del dolor
en Jovellanos.

Octubre imprescindible

IMMEMORIAL HUMUS

In Jovellanos, the flower of Jericho.
Mother, who find your womb
among shackles and straps,
this is your beach.

The white sky pierced by the rays.
The greyish sea of the hold
fiercely casting out
gagged blacks,
throwing them,
through the fog,
onto any old port.

Girl, mother who find your womb
among wild beasts and bones,
look at the warder,
overseer of your steps,
consuming himself,
surrounded and a prisoner.

Beasts of burden we were.

In the plains of Jovellanos,
the flower of Jericho.
Oh plains of pain
in Jovellanos.

Indispensable October

SALTIMBANQUIS

Vamos, Brígida; vámonos.
Apaguemos las luces de la comarca.
Alcancemos a nuestros saltimbanquis.
Allá los diviso, ladeando el borde
de Ciego de Avila. El sudor
de sus ropas está presente
como su misma compañía,

-¿Y esós quiénes son?-,
me preguntarás enseguida,
curiosa de todo como nunca,
-Son meras figuras andariegas, almas vivas,
brujos, cantores, talabarteros, cómicos de la legua,
traídos desde muy lejos,
recién azotados en el pueblo
por el que acaban de transitar y vivir.
Vamos con ellos. Bebamos de sus jícaras-,
te diré, simplemente.

Partimos con la mojiganga alborotada.
Nuestras filas desbordando injurias,
cepos, alacranes, iruques, culebras,
yucas, flautas, pájaros, yagrumas.

Y con la paciencia de Brígida,
ay, en amasijo,
fuimos todos andando por la inmensa
llanura. Así que
fieras y soldados comenzaron a perseguirnos.

Travelling Circus

Let's go, Brígida, let's go.
Let's put out the lights of the district
Let's go up to our travelling circus.
There I see them, turning the outskirts
of Ciego de Avila. The sweat
of their clothes is present
like their very company.

"And who are these?"
you will ask me immediately,
curious about everything as ever,
"They're mere wandering figures, living souls,
sorcerers, singers, leather-workers, comedians,
brought from very far,
recently whipped in the village
through which they have passed and lived.
Let's go with them. Let's drink from their calabashes",
I'll tell you, simply.

We went off with the stirred up mummery.
Our files flowing over insults,
traps, scorpions, iruques, snakes,
manioc, flutes, birds, yagruma trees.

And with the patience of Brígida,
ay, in a mass,
we all went walking through the immense
plain. Thus
wild beasts and soldiers began to pursue us.

Por fin, casi diezmados, degollaron nuestras vacas.
¡Qué pena tan incierta!

Dejamos nuestros huesos a su paso,
a la luz de la mañana,
ya entrando a Camagüey.

Octubre imprescindible

In the end, almost decimated, they cut the throats of
our cows.
What uncertain suffering!

We left our bones in their way,
in the morning light,
already coming into Camagüey.

Indispensable October

Negro

Tu pelo,
para algunos,
era diablura del infierno;
pero el zunzún allí
puso su nido, sin reparos,
cuando pendías en lo alto del horcón,
frente al palacio
                    de los capitanes.
Dijeron, sí, que el polvo del camino
te hizo infiel y violáceo,
como esas flores invernales
del trópico, siempre
tan asombrosas y arrogantes.
                    Ya moribundo
sospechan que tu sonrisa era salobre
y tu musgo impalpable para el encuentro del amor.
Otros afirman que tus palos de monte
nos trajeron ese daño sombrío
que no nos deja relucir ante Europa
y que nos lanza, en la vorágine ritual,
a ese ritmo imposible
de los tambores innombrables.
Nosotros amaremos por siempre
tus huellas y tu ánimo de bronce
porque has traído esa luz viva del pasado
fluyente,
ese dolor de haber entrado limpio a la batalla,

BLACK MAN

Your hair,
for some,
was devilry from the Inferno;
but the hummingbird built his nest
there, with no misgivings,
when you were hanging high on the gallows post,
in front of the palace
                    of the captains.
They said, yes, that the dust of the road
made you disloyal and purplish,
like those winter flowers
of the tropics, always
so dazzling and arrogant.
                    Then dying
they suspected that your smile was salty
and your moss impalpable for the encounter of love.
Others affirmed that your swamp sticks
brought us that sombre damage
which does not allow us to shine before Europe
and which hurls us, in the ritual maelstrom,
into that impossible rhythm
of unnameable drums.
We will always love
your tracks and your bronze spirit
because you have brought that living light of the
                                        flowing
past,
that pain of having entered clean into the battle,

ese afecto sencillo por las campanas y los ríos,
ese rumor de aliento libre en primavera
que corre al mar para volver
y volver a partir.

Piedra pulida

that simple affection for bells and rivers,
that rumour of breath free in the Spring
which runs to the sea in order to return
and leave all over again.

Polished Stone

HABLANDO CON UNA CULEBRA

A ti también te dieron con un palo,
te estrujaron y te escupieron, te pisotearon siempre;
a ti, te mataron con delicia
y te echaron una maldición que hasta hoy hicieron
                                        cumplir.
No digas tú que en la hora de la queja
fuiste más poseedora que Angélica, mi madre.

Mas cuando entre sicomoros e hicacos
hayas iniciado tu majomía irredenta,
recuerda bien el acíbar de tus verdugos,
pon atención a las lágrimas y no a su llanto,
pon atención al puñal y no a su empuñadura,
desoye la oración y la sorda palabra del Señor
y rodéanos después de una sola mirada,
que ya te alcanzaremos animada,
y cuando despiertes de tu sueño, continuada tu estirpe,
sacúdete, pega, muerde y mata tú también
que ya vuelas y vives en tu justo lugar.

Octubre imprescindible

SPEAKING TO A SNAKE

They beat you too with a stick,
they wrung you and they spat on you, they trampled
on you always;
you they killed with delight
and they put a curse on you which even today they
have carried through.
Don't you say that at the hour of the complaint
you were more the possessor than Angélica, my
mother.

But when in between sycamores and coco plumtrees
you have begun your irredentist lament
remember well the aloes of your torturers,
pay attention to the tears and not to their wailing,
pay attention to the dagger and not to its hilt,
don't listen to the prayer and the dull word of the Lord
and encircle us after with a single look,
for we will then reach you excited,
and when you wake from your dream, your lineage
continued,
shake yourself, hit, bite, and kill, you as well
for you now fly and live in your proper place.

Indispensable October

El Loto y el Café

En la misma ciudad,
cuando la noche va a caer,
aparecen dos esclavas muy viejas, apertrechadas
en la volanta de su ama, con loto del Oriente
y café de Santiago. Las dos esclavas están
en el vehículo, y sin embargo necesitan el sol,
necesitan el alba. Una, va a descender de la volanta
porque quiere mirar a las estrellas.
La segunda, prefiere caminar hasta llegar a la plaza
más vieja.

Richard trajo su flauta

THE LOTUS AND THE COFFEE

In the same city,
when night is about to fall,
two very old slaves appear, furnished
in their mistress's carriage, with lotus from the Orient
and coffee from Santiago. The two slaves are
in the vehicle, and even so they need the sun,
they need the dawn. One, is going to get out of the
carriage
because she wants to look at the stars.
The second, prefers to carry on until she gets to the
oldest square.

Richard Brought His Flute

Güijes

Saliendo el sol de la mañana
miramos al espejo silvestre
donde espigan la cueva provincial
y el aroma silente de las hierbas.
Y ya daban las seis en la existencia
real del día.
                    Lo decían
el agua de los saltos
y el campanario viejo junto al río,
entre el rumor de aquel desfiladero.
Corrieron a su encuentro los güijes, otra vez,
y en la noche tan joven, zarparon
en un solo relámpago de luz...

Octubre imprescindible

GÜIJES

As the morning sun comes out
we look at the wild mirror
where the provincial cave
and the silent aroma of the grasses spring up.
And six o'clock was already sounding in the real
existence of the day.
            The water of the cascades
and the old bell-tower by the river
were saying it,
amid the rumour of that ravine.
The *güijes* ran to meet it, once again,
and in the night so young, they set sail
in a single flash of light...

Indispensable October

MADRIGAL PARA CIMARRONES

A Miguel Barnet

La cabeza y las manos colgadas, llameantes,
burlando el rastro del Perseguidor.
Los cuerpos sudorosos se lanzan a la manigua
          húmeda.
Qué belleza tan dura tienen sus corazones.
Sobre sus machetes, como sobre ramales,
anidan palomas y jutías,
y el tiempo de sol,
y el tiempo de luna,
y el tiempo de la voluntad
haciéndolos renacer como a niños,
como a dulces niños de una libertad ya conquistada.

Octubre imprescindible

MADRIGAL FOR MAROONS

To Miguel Barnet

Their heads and hands hanging, flaming,
confusing the trail for the Tracker.
The sweaty bodies throw themselves into the wet
      swamp.
What a hard beauty their hearts have.
On their machetes, as on branches,
doves and jutias nest,
and the time of sun,
and the time of moon,
and the time of will
making them reborn as if they were children,
as if they were sweet children of a liberty already won.

Indispensable October

Niño con los Ojos Rosados

Caminando,
empujados quizás por una brisa,
hemos llegado a los extremos
de la bullicie comercial.
Las estatuas de mármol
condensándose en el atardecer.
Ver al turista
parpadeando, dormido,
ante el insólito profundo chorro azul
de las ballenas. Y las lanchas hirvientes
y los hirvientes arrecifes
sobre el fuego mortal.
Un alto negro inmenso
cruza el portal en sombras
y junto a la cadera
su negra inmensa y alta
va cruzando también.
Entre los dos,
como entre cielo y tierra,
como entre luna y sol,
un cochecito débil
circunda la alameda.
Allá dentro, vivaz,
un niño con los ojos rosados
se acurruca entre encajes
mientras contempla, puro,
la azul bahía letal.

Piedra pulida

Child with Pink Eyes

Walking,
pushed perhaps by a breeze,
we have arrived at the extremes
of the commercial hubbub.
The marble statues
becoming covered in condensation in the dusk.
Seeing the tourist
blinking, asleep,
in front of the out-of-the-ordinary blue deep jet
of the whales. And the boiling launches
and the boiling reefs
on the mortal fire.
A tall immense black man
comes through the gate in shadow
and at his side
his immense and tall black woman
is coming as well.
Between the two,
as if between sky and land,
as if between moon and sun,
a weak little push chair
goes around the avenue.
There in it, lively,
a child with pink eyes
curls up in lace
while he contemplates, pure,
the lethal blue bay.

Polished Stone

Los Ojos de Eleggua

esta noche
junto a las puertas del caserón rojizo
he vuelto a ver los ojos del guerrero
eleggua
la lengua
roja de sangre como el corazón de los hierros
los pies dorados desiguales
la tez de fuego el pecho encabritado y sonriente

acaba de estallar en gritos
eleggua salta
imagina los cantos
roza el espacio con un puñal de cobre
quién le consentirá
si no es la piedra
o el coco blanco
quién recogerá los caracoles de sus ojos

ya no sabrá de Olofi si ha perdido el camino
ya no sabrá de los rituales
ni de los animales en su honor
ni de la lanza mágica
ni de los silbidos en la noche

si los ojos de eleggua regresaran
volverían a atravesar el río pujante
donde los dioses se alejaban donde existían los peces
quién sabrá entonces del cantar de los pájaros
el gran eleggua ata mis manos

THE EYES OF ELEGGUA

tonight
by the doors of the big reddish house
I have seen again the eyes of the warrior
eleggua
his tongue
red with blood like the heart of iron
his golden unequal feet
his skin of fire his chest thrust out and smiling

he has just erupted in cries
eleggua jumps
imagines the songs
brushes the space with a fist of copper
who will give in to him
if it is not stone
nor the white coconut
who will gather the snails of his eyes

now he will not know if of Olofi he has lost the way
now he will not know of the rituals
nor of the animals in his honour
nor of the magic lance
nor of the whistles in the night

if the eyes of eleggua were to come back
they would cross again the mighty river
where the gods used to go away to where the fish existed
who will know then about the song of the birds
the great eleggua ties my hands

y las abre y ya huye
y bajo la yagruma está el secreto
las cabezas el sol y lo que silba
como único poder del oscuro camino

Richard trajo su flauta

and opens them and now flees
and under the yagruma tree is the secret
the heads the sun and what whistles
like the only power of the dark path

Richard Brought His Flute

Para Escapar Herido

a Rogelio Martínez Furé

Sucede que es la noche, compañero,
y Ochún sola, tan sola
–o Mercedes, o Carmen, o María–
busca donde la luna brilla;
se va a guardar detrás del adoquín del patio,
se va a guardar su amor al bosque negro, al vino;
sucede, salta entonces un ciervo de sus brazos
y sangra sangra entonces el ciervo de la diosa,
para escapar herido a donde nadie
para escapar herido, para escapar herido.

Richard trajo su flauta

In Order to Escape Wounded

To Rogelio Martínez Furé

It turns out that it is night time, companion,
and Ochún, on her own, so alone
-or Mercedes, or Carmen, or María-
is searching where the moon shines;
she is going to hide herself behind the paving stones
                                          of the patio,
she is going to hide her love in the black wood, in
                                          the wine;
it turns out, a stag then leaps out of her arms
and then the stag of the goddess bleeds bleeds,
in order to escape wounded to where there is nobody
to escape wounded, to escape wounded.

Richard Brought His Flute

AMO A MI AMO

Amo a mi amo.
Recojo leña para encender su fuego cotidiano.
Amo sus ojos claros.
Mansa cual un cordero
esparzo gotas de miel por sus orejas.
Amo sus manos
que me depositaron sobre un lecho de hierbas:
Mi amo muerde y subyuga.
Me cuenta historias sigilosas mientras
abanico todo su cuerpo cundido de llagas y balazos,
de días de sol y guerra de rapiña.
Amo sus pies que piratearon y rodaron
por tierras ajenas.
Los froto con los polvos más finos
que encontré, una mañana,
saliendo de la vega.
Tañó la vihuela y de su garganta salían
coplas sonoras, como nacidas de la garganta de
                                        Manrique.

Yo quería haber oído una marímbula sonar.
Amo su boca roja, fina,
desde donde van saliendo palabras
que no alcanzo a descifrar
todavía. Mi lengua para él ya no es la suya.

Y la seda del tiempo hecha trizas.

I LOVE MY MASTER

I love my master.
I gather wood to light his daily fire.
I love his light eyes.
Gentle as a lamb
I spread drops of honey on his ears.
I love his hands
which laid me on a bed of grasses:
My master bites and subjugates.
He tells me stealthy stories while
I fan his whole body pitted with blade and shot wounds,
by days of sun and war of rapine.
I love his feet which went pirating and wandered
through alien lands.
I rub them with the finest powders
which I found, one morning,
coming out of the tobacco plantation.
He plucked the vihuela and from his throat came
couplets sonorous as if born from the throat of
Manrique.

I would love to have heard a marimbula.
I love his red, fine mouth,
from which words come out
which I cannot manage to decipher
yet. My tongue for him is even now not his own.

And the silk of time turned to shreds.

Oyendo hablar a los viejos guardieros, supe
que mi amor
da latigazos en las calderas del ingenio,
como si fueran un infierno, el de aquel Señor Dios
de quien me hablaba sin cesar.

¿Qué me dirá?
¿Por qué vivo en la morada ideal para un murciélago?
¿Por qué le sirvo?
¿Adonde va en su espléndido coche
tirado por caballos más felices que yo?
Mi amor es como la maleza que cubre la dotación,
única posesión inexpugnable mía.

Maldigo

esta bata de muselina que me ha impuesto;
estos encajes vanos que despiadado me endilgó;
estos quehaceres para mí en el atardecer sin girasoles;
esta lengua abigarradamente hostil que no mastico;
estos senos de piedra que no pueden siquiera
                                    amamantarlo;
este vientre rajado por su látigo inmemorial;
este maldito corazón.

Amo a mi amo pero todas las noches,
cuando atravieso la vereda florida hacia el cañaveral
        donde a hurtadillas hemos hecho el amor,
me veo cuchillo en mano, desollándole como a una res
        sin culpa.

Listening to the old warders speak, I knew
that my love
uses the lash in the cauldrons of the sugarmill,
as if they were an inferno, the one of that Lord God
of whom he used to speak to me unceasingly.

What would he say to me?
Why do I live in the ideal dwelling for a bat?
Why do I serve him?
Where does he go in his splendid coach
pulled by horses happier than I?
My love is like the undergrowth which covers the estate
the only possession inexpugnably mine.

I curse

this muslin gown he has imposed on me;
these vain pieces of lace with which he pitilessly
                                        encumbered me;
these tasks for me in the dusk without sunflowers;
this gaudily hostile language which I cannot chew;
these breasts of stone which cannot even suckle him;
this womb torn by his immemorial whip;
this accursed heart.

I love my master but every night,
when I cross the flower-bordered path towards the
                                        plantation
            where, surreptitiously, we have made love,
I see myself knife in hand, slaughtering him as I would
                                              a beast
            without guilt.

Ensordecedores toques de tambor ya no me dejan
oír ni sus quebrantos, ni sus quejas.
Las campanas me llaman...

Octubre imprescindible

Deafening drumbeats now don't allow me
to hear either his suffering, or his complaints.
The bells call me...

Indispensable October

La Rebambaramba

La farola, el ciempiés,
la brújula del tacto
y la comparsa
disuelta hacia el volcán.

Cinturas y cinturas
como puentes colgantes;
jardineras y dandys
sonriendo en la alameda.

La sombrilla en la mano,
la volanta prendida,
el sapo en el portal,
el calesero impávido,
la tumba abierta y cálida,
en el solar perdido.

El cuchillo en la noche,
la tropelía y la clave,
los metales y el hierro,
la furia firme del final.

¿Dónde está
la corneta del loco?

¿Dónde afila su arma
el bastonero de Santiago?

THE REBAMBARAMBA

The streetlight, the centipede,
the divination of touch
and the masquerade
dispersed towards the volcano.

Waists and waists
like hanging bridges;
dungarees and dandys
smiling in the avenue.

The umbrella in the hand,
the carriage tethered,
the frog in the doorway,
the impassive calash-driver,
the tomb open and warm,
in the lost plot of land.

The knife in the night,
the outrage and the key,
the metals and the steel,
the firm fury of the end.

Where is
the madman's cornet?

Where does the Santiago
Drum Major edge his weapon?

¿Dónde canta,
señor, el mantón de Ma'Luisa?

¿Y Caridad y Pastora?

¿Dónde canta la conga
su tonada mejor?

Tango, tango real.

Todos
somos hermanos.

Elogio de la danza

Where, sir,
does Ma' Luisa's shawl sing?

And Caridad and Pastora?

Where does the conga
sing its best tune?

Tango, true tango.

We are all
brothers.

Eulogy of the Dance

Elogio de Nieves Fresneda

Como un pez volador: Nieves Fresneda.

Olas de mar, galeotes,
azules pétalos de algas
cubren sus días y sus horas,
renaciendo a sus pies.

Un rumor de Benin
la trajo al fondo de esta tierra.

Allí están
sus culebras,
sus círculos,
sus cauris,
sus sayas,
sus pies,
buscando la manigua,
abriendo rutas desconocidas
hacia Olókun.

Sus pies marítimos,
al fin,
troncos de sal,
perpetuos pies de Nieves,
alzados como lunas para Yemayá.

Y en el espacio,
luego,
entre la espuma,

EULOGY FOR NIEVES FRESNEDA

Like a flying fish: Nieves Fresneda.

Sea waves, galleons,
blue petals of algae
cover her days and her hours,
born again at her feet.

A rumour from Benin
brought her to the depths of this country.

There are
her snakes,
her circles,
her cowries,
her skirts,
her feet,
looking for the jungle,
opening unknown routes
to Olókun.

Her maritime feet,
in the end,
logs of salt,
the perpetual feet of Nieves,
raised like moons for Yemayá.

And in the space,
later,
in the foam,

Nieves
girando sobre el mar,
Nieves por entre el canto
inmemorial del sueño,
Nieves
en los mares de Cuba,
Nieves.

Elogio de la danza

Nieves
gyrating over the sea,
Nieves between the immemorial
song of the dream,
Nieves
in the seas of Cuba,
Nieves.

Eulogy of the Dance

Merceditas

(A la memoria de Merceditas Valdés)
para Luis Carbonell

Mírenla como va de amarillo
igual que el girasol
y la yema
y el trigo.
Colibrí perfumado
va su pie diminuto
bordando el adoquín
adormecido.

Mírenla como va
cantando a solas
en un barquito
de miel y calabazas.
Y las abejas desoladas
dibujando su rostro
renacido.

Merceditas
—grita la luna blanca—.
Merceditas
no es una sombra inesperada
no es una sombra nunca
ni es un sueño
sino una voz recien cortada
pero qué voz

MERCEDITAS

(To the memory of Merceditas Valdés)
for Luis Carbonell

Look at her as she goes in yellow
the same as a sunflower
and egg-yolk
and wheat.
A perfumed hummingbird
her diminutive foot
goes along embroidering the dozing
paving stone.

Look at her as she goes
singing by herself
in a little boat
of honey and pumpkins.
And the desolate bees
drawing her reborn
face.

Merceditas
—shouts the white moon—.
Merceditas
is not an unexpected shade
is never a shade
nor is a dream
but a newly-cut voice
but what a voice,

pero qué sombra.
Qué sueño entrecortado.
Merceditas
—vuelve a gritar la luna blanca—.

Mírenla como va de amarillo
igual que el girasol
y la yema
 y el trigo.
Colibrí perfumado,
va su pie diminuto
bordando el adoquín
adormecido.

Montada sobre un pavo real de espumas
va cabalgando sobre Cuba.
Mírenla bien.
Mírenla aquí
en su coral de soles fijos,
en su coral de plumas sacras,
en su fulgor de alcoholes sabios,
en su esplendor de pulseras dormidas.
Merceditas
—grita la luna enardecida—.

Mírenla como va de amarillo
igual que el girasol
y la yema
y el trigo.
Colibrí perfumado,
va su pie diminuto

but what a shade.
What an interrupted dream.
Merceditas
—the white moon shouts again—.

Look at her as she goes in yellow
the same as a sunflower
and egg-yolk
and wheat.
A perfumed hummingbird
her diminutive foot
goes along embroidering the dozing
paving stone.

Mounted on a peacock of foam
she goes riding over Cuba.
Look at her well.
Look at her here
in her coral of fixed suns,
in her coral of sacred plumes,
in her brilliance of wise alcohols,
in her splendour of sleeping bracelets.
Merceditas
—shouts the impassioned moon—.

Look at her as she goes in yellow
the same as a sunflower
and egg-yolk
and wheat.
A perfumed hummingbird
her diminutive foot

bordando el adoquín
adormecido
y un manto de oro fino
cayendo para siempre
entre las aguas breves del río.

(inédito)

goes along embroidering the dozing
paving stone
and a cloak of fine gold
falling forever
into the shallow waters of the river.

(unpublished)

Pareja Negra

Pasos en el océano
con ansias de baobab,
desde las aguas turbias
que ya no son azules;
pasos que nos alzan su voz,
más allá de la espuma.

Hombre y mujer,
sobre el océano,
entre los aires mismos
de la nada,
de su alma acostumbrada
al vaivén de los ríos,
a la carne sonora
de su ébano,
a la flácida luz
del monte umbrío
que los entoma
en su torno infinito.

Mujer y hombre
lado a lado
del bosque o la montaña,
del maguey a la luna,
con lanzas en los labios,
con el ojo de buey
entre las manos,
con un manto elegiaco
para cada pupila,

BLACK COUPLE

Steps in the ocean
longing for a baobab tree,
from the turgid waters
which are no longer blue;
steps which raise their voice to us,
beyond the foam.

Man and woman,
on the ocean,
between the very air
of nothingness,
of their soul accustomed
to the ebb and flow of rivers,
to the sonorous flesh
of their ebony,
to the flaccid light
of the shadowed mountain
which surrounds them
in its infinite turning.

Man and woman
side by side
with the forest or the mountain,
with the agave or the moon,
with lances in their lips,
with the ox eye
in their hands,
with an elegiac cloak
for each pupil of the eye,

con un árbol de paz,
entre los dos.

Elogio de la danza

with a tree of peace,
between the two.

Eulogy of the Dance

Mundos

Mi casa es un gran barco
que no desea emprender su travesía.
Sus mástiles, sus jarcias,
se tornaron raíces
y medusas plantadas en medio de la mar;
a estas alturas,
¿podré decir el mar
oteado por el sol
o por el oro fétido del galeón desollado?

Mi casa es un gran barco
que resguarda la noche.
Quiero los vinos leves de su espuma.
Quiero los hierros fuertes de sus corrales.
Quiero, al fin, la lenta y prístina llanura
derramada en los ojos.
Oh los ojos furtivos del pasado mortal.

Mi casa es un gran barco
rodeado de aguas nuevas
donde clavo mis manos
y las pupilas que he traído.
Bailar, bogar, llorar y andar
entre los peces de cubierta.
Viejo mundo el que amo,
nuevo mundo el que amo,
mundos, mundos los dos, mis mundos:
Oh las tortugas sacras;
ay, las algas;

WORLDS

My house is a great ship
which does not want to undertake its crossing.
Its masts, its rigging,
turned themselves into roots
and jellyfish planted in the middle of the sea;
at this stage,
can I say the sea
scanned by the sun
or by the foetid gold of the shattered galleon?

My house is a great ship
which safeguards the night.
I am fond of the light wines of its foam.
I am fond of the strong iron of its pens.
I am fond, in the end, of the slow and pristine plain
spilled in its eyes.
Oh the furtive eyes of the mortal past.

My house is a great ship
surrounded by new waters
into which I dig my hands
and the pupils of the eyes I have brought.
Dancing, rowing, crying and walking
among the fish on deck.
Old world the one I love,
new world the one I love,
worlds, worlds the two, my worlds:
Oh the sacred tortoises;
ay, the algae;

ah el nombre de la mujer costeña,
anclada en el centro de un mundo.

Vivo en el sesgo tallado de la espiga.

"Vamos a andar," me dijo alguna vez,
con su aliento amoroso, aquel esclavo.
Y ambos sembramos nuestras piernas
como troncos incólumes, como nidos fundados;
abrazándonos bajo la tempestad.
"Piensa en el tiempo de la piedra pulida
que siempre llega aquí
para lanzar el arco y otra vez el origen,"
volvió a decirme
y ya su alma dejaba de estar sola,
y ya su boca misma era una isla ardorosa,
harta de frutas, lenguas, olas y pergaminos.
Mi casa es un gran barco
sin demonios apenas
porque los conminé a la retirada;
porque quiero la dicha como regla suprema;
como regla suprema quiero el violín,
la contradanza ilesa en su vaivén

Mi casa es un gran barco
y trazo con mis venas el mapamundi nunca
            visto
de los islotes a mi diestra
Vivo en mi casa que es un barco
(qué poderoso barco me cobija)
Vivo en mi casa que es un barco
(qué poderosa espuma me refresca)

ah the name of the coastal woman,
anchored in the centre of a world.

I live in the carved bias of the masthead.

"Let's go far a walk," that slave,
with his loving breath, once said to me.
And we both sowed our legs
like undamaged trunks, like established nests;
embracing each other beneath the storm.
"Think of the time of the polished stone
which always arrives here
in order to throw the arch and once more the origin,"
he said to me again
and by then his soul stopped being on its own,
and by then his very mouth was a burning island,
laden with fruit, tongues, waves and parchments.
My house is a great ship
without any demons hardly
because I ordained their retreat;
because I want good fortune as a supreme rule;
as a supreme rule I want the violin,
the unscathed counterdance in its coming and going.

My house is a great ship
and I trace with my veins the mapamundi never
                    seen
of the islets on my right.
I live in my house which is a ship
(what a powerful boat shelters me)
I live in my house which is a ship
(what powerful foam refreshes me)

Vivo en mi barco vivo
amparada del trueno y la centella
Mi casa es un gran barco
digo
sobre la isla dorada
en que voy a morir

Piedra pulida

I live in my living boat
shielded from thunder and lightning
My house is a great ship
I say
on the golden island
on which I am going to die

Polished Stone

MADRE

Mi madre no tuvo jardín
sino islas acantiladas
flotando, bajo el sol,
en sus corales delicados.
No hubo una rama limpia
en su pupila sino muchos garrotes.
Qué tiempo aquel cuando corría, descalza,
sobre la cal de los orfelinatos
y no sabía reír
y no podía siquiera mirar el horizonte.
Ella no tuvo el aposento de marfil,
ni la sala de mimbre,
ni el vitral silencioso del trópico.
Mi madre tuvo el canto y el pañuelo
para acunar la fe de mis entrañas,
para alzar su cabeza de reina desoída
y dejarnos sus manos, como piedras preciosas,
frente a los restos fríos del enemigo.

Piedra pulida

MOTHER

My mother didn't have a garden
only cliff-edged islands
floating, under the sun,
on their delicate coral.
There was no clean branch
in the pupil of her eye only lots of garottes.
What a time that was when she used to run, barefoot,
on the whitewash of the orphanages
and she didn't know how to laugh
and she couldn't even look at the horizon.
She didn't have the ivory bedroom
nor the wicker-furnished drawing-room,
nor the silent stained-glass of the tropics.
My mother had her singing and the scarf
to rock the faith of my insides,
to lift up her head of an unheard queen,
and leave us her hands, like precious stones,
in the face of the cold remains of the enemy.

Polished Stone

A LA SOMBRA DE LOS TRANVÍAS

A Eliseo Diego

A la sombra de los tranvías
abuela, ¿traía recogida una trenza
o era el relato familiar
quien lo afirmaba?
Mi pobre abuela... que nunca vi.

Piedra pulida

In the Shadow of the Trams

To Eliseo Diego

In the shadow of the trams
grandmother, did she wear a plait pinned up
or was it the family story
which said so?
My poor grandmother... whom I never saw.

Polished Stone

Richard Trajo Su Flauta

I

sin el menor ruido
con las venas del cognac y el danzón de Romeu
se apoderaba abuelo Egües de un sillón patidifuso y
tieso
"ya no queda ningún músico de mi
generación en Placetas
sobre todo la banda una retreta mala como cará"
estamos todos juntos pero no llega el esperado
y llueve mucho fuera de la casa

cada noche reaparecen
los relatos de Juan Gualberto en la nación antigua
como el aliento de los árboles

mientras revolvíamos los discos

"la batería es lo que lleva el suin"

truena y llueve
y llueve para ahogarnos a todos con
nuestros respectivos
catorce o quince años
ahí la muerte y luego ¿dónde estaremos todos?
miramos por la ventana frente a la estrecha calle
de la iglesia de San Nicolás
(nunca nos gustaron los curas)
es la hora de comida y picamos el pan
y tomamos cerveza

RICHARD BROUGHT HIS FLUTE

I

without the smallest noise
with the veins of the cognac and the dance of Romeu
grandfather Egües was getting into an upright, splay-
                                    legged chair
            "now there is no musician of my
            generation in Placetas
            above all the band a group disgracefully bad"
we are all together but the one who is expected hasn't
                                    arrived
and it rains a lot outside the house

every night
the stories of Juan Gualberto in the old natio reappear
like the breath of the trees

while we spin the discs

"the drums are what carries the swing"

it thunders and rains
            and rains to drown all of us at our respective
            fourteen or fifteen years
there's death and after where will we all be?
we look through the window onto the narrow street
of the church of St Nicholas
(we never liked priests)
it's dinner time and we pick at the bread
and drink beer.

II

el piano está en la sala

la oportunidad del piano en la sala
bastaba para que distinguiéramos
todo lo demás
toda la sala no es grande sólo el lugar del piano
"¿qué te parece si oímos un poco de música?"

allí acudimos todos sin excepción

las buenas tardes o las buenas noches
embargan el pensamiento
estamos juntos todos ¿qué más?
juntos únicamente
aunque el cuerpo irritado de abuelo Egües
sus espejuelos
quieran acolcharnos y enseñarnos
todos los golpes de la flauta
además del solfeo

y buena sangre por supuesto hace falta
para atender las notas musicales
y sin saber por qué
la lejanía y la atención de uno o varios de nosotros
se hacen patentes a esta hora
a este instante de sonido y disciplina secular

el piano está en la sala

II

the piano is in the living-room

the opportunity of the piano in the living-room
was enough for us to be able to distinguish
everything else
the whole of the living-room is not big only the
                              place where the piano is
"what about listening to a little music?"

we all went there without exception

the good afternoons or the good nights
seize thought
we are all together, what else?
together only
even though the irritated body of grandfather Egües
his spectacles
would like to cosset us and show us
all the sounds of the flute
as well as scales

and good blood is of course necessary
in order to pay attention to the notes
and without knowing why
the distance and the attention of one or some of us
become patent at this point
at this instant of sound and secular discipline

the piano is in the living-room

(es lunes y algunos de nosotros ha encendido su vela
      gran vela semanal para eleggua
      no hay nada que decir
sólo tomar una botella de ron al lado de la puerta)

todos virtuosos y de buenas costumbres
las niñas con las manos cruzadas
los niños practicando solfeo
refunfuñando del violín pegajoso y alcohólico

la pequeñez de todos nuestros actos se resumía
en saber si reconocíamos fácilmente un cuadro de
                      Picasso
si los latinos si los negros vivían mejor en Nueva
                      York

habíamos comprado por encargo del primo mayor
a Count Basie, Duke Ellington y el trío Nat Cole
y era posible obtener para diciembre
el concierto para flauta de Mozart

en toda la maravilla de la sala descansa el piano

una serpiente se levanta ahora al caer la noche

es el momento

la aparición de los relatos

(it's Monday and some of us have lit our candle
        the big weekly candle for eleggua
        there is nothing to say
only drink a bottle of rum beside the door)

all virtuous and of good habits
the girls with their hands folded
the boys practising scales
rumbling on the sticky and alcoholic violin

the smallness of all our acts summed itself up
in knowing if we could easily recognise a painting
                        by Picasso
if the Latinos if the Blacks lived better in New York

we had bought through our eldest cousin
Count Basie, Duke Ellington and the Nat Cole Trio
and it was possible to get for December
the Mozart Flute Concerto

in the whole marvel of the drawing-room the piano
                                 rests

a serpent rises now as night falls

it is the moment

the appearance of the stories

VIII

los orishas nunca se hicieron eco de nuestras voces
        sabíamos que rondaban la casa
y que amedentraban como güijes toda la maldición
alguien estaba o residía
        soberanamente
un simple palo o bejuco era su atmósfera
soplar por él con toda la fuerza de un negro
        enamorado

los orishas oscilaban tranquilos alrededor de los dedos
los dedos de la mano derecha disminuían el ritmo
        lentamente
el esperado trae su flauta

todos pedíamos su presencia alrededor de la mesa
        caoba
el oro del hogar se derrumbó sobre sus hombros
        misteriosamente
maravilloso estar entre nosotros Richard
        con esa flauta sola

Richard trajo su flauta

VIII

the orishas never turned themselves into the echo of
                                        our voices
            we knew they circled the house
and that they infused the whole malediction with
                                    terror like *güijes*
someone was or resided
            sovereignly
a simple stick or liana was his atmosphere
blowing through it with all the force of a black
                                    man in love

the orishas oscillated quietly around the fingers
the fingers of the right hand diminished the rhythm
            slowly
he who is expected brings his flute

we all asked for his presence around the mahogany
                                        table
the gold of the hearth fire poured itself onto his
                                        shoulders
            mysteriously
it was marvellous that Richard was among us
            with that solo flute.

                        Richard Brought His Flute

Restos del Coral Island

"Esa chatarra que se ve en la orilla
son los restos del Coral Island,"
decía mi padre
hechizado por las columnas de luz blanca
que levitaban de los huecos rojizos
que tal vez sirvieron de anteojos
a la proa de ese gran transatlántico
que dice mi padre era el Coral Island.
Vamos sentados en un ómnibus cotidiano,
rápido y caluroso como este mes de julio de 1986.
No quise preguntarle porque me dio un vuelco el
corazón.
Un zumbido de mariposas también me impidió hacer
preguntas.
Mi padre me miró de un modo peculiar.
¿Habíamos entrado los dos
a reconocemos en aquel himno del pasado?
Mi padre y yo mirándonos sin decir nada.
Yo sólo tenía oídos para escuchar el chirriar de las
olas
contra los hierros tutelares del Coral Island.
Y pensé en una historia de amor,
en una pasión desmoronada sobre dientes de perro y
espuma de mar.
Una loca pasión bien muerta,
fenecida,
de la que ni siquiera se desprende ya
una columna de luz blanca
ni el portento a la vista que se llamó,

REMAINS OF THE CORAL ISLAND

"That scrap-heap which you can see at the water's
                                                        edge
is the remains of the Coral Island",
my father used to say
bewitched by the columns of white light
which levitated out of the reddish portholes
which maybe served as eyeglasses
on the prow of the great transatlantic liner
which my father says was the Coral Island.
We go seated in an everyday bus,
rapid and warm like this month of July of 1986.
I didn't want to ask him questions because my heart
                                                        jumped inside me.
A humming of butterflies also prevented me from
                                                        asking questions.
My father looked at me in a peculiar way.
Had we two begun
to recognise each other in that hymn of the past?
My father and I looking at each other without saying
                                                        anything.
I only had ears to listen to the screech of the waves
against the tutelary metal of the Coral Island.
And I thought about a love story,
a passion broken on dogs' teeth and sea foam.
A mad passion truly dead,
expired
from which neither a column of white light
nor the portent to the eye which was called,
some time, the Coral Island,

alguna vez, el Coral Island.
"Esa chatarra que se ve en la orilla
son los restos del Coral Island,"
decía mi padre sin mirarme.

Paisaje célebre

has yet disentangled itself.
"That scrap-heap which you can see at the water's
edge
is the remains of the Coral Island"
my father said without looking at me.

Famous Landscape

Un Patio de la Habana

A Gerardo Fulleda León

Un patio de La Habana,
como pedía Machado,
es caro a la memoria.
Sin altos muros,
sin esa lumbre intrépida
del arcoiris,
sin la flor andaluza
que tanto abuela reclamaba
en los búcaros...

Un patio de La Habana
conserva huesos de los muertos
porque ellos son anchos tesoros,
viejas semillas de labrador.

Un patio, ay, de donde sale
tanta estrella.

Piedra pulida

A Patio in Havana

To Gerardo Fulleda León

A patio in Havana
like Machado used to ask for
is dear to the memory.
Without high walls,
without that intrepid glow
of the rainbow,
without the Andalusian flower
which grandmother insisted on so much
in the vases...

A patio in Havana
keeps the bones of the dead
because they are ample treasures
old seeds of a labourer.

A patio, ay, out of which comes
so much starlight.

Polished Stone

POGOLOTTI

Para Graziella, por supuesto

Antes de ser el nombre de un pintor,
de un gran pintor cubano,
Pogolotti, en mi infancia,
era una rústica ruta de malezas
que conducía a una casona alta,
larga y profunda,
con un patio de cercas de madera
acartonado por calabazas y yagrumas lentas
y un olor excitante a chilindrón de chivo.
En Pogolotti pasé tantos domingos
de quimbombó bajo los mangos,
de azúcares y miel para recién nacidos,
de "no se vayan todavía
que ahorita viene Silvio para que vea a las niñas."
Todo cantaba al mediodía
cuando las chimeneas de las pequeñas fábricas
ascendían con sus humos
como una plegaria contra la intemperie
y la necesidad escondida.
Me abrazaba madrina
y yo miraba hacia la calle sin asfaltar
mientras pasaban los estibadores sin empleo,
los estibadores fustigados por el silbido industrial
            del *ferry* en los muelles.
Como en los murales mexicanos,
el aire se hacía aristas,

POGOLOTTI

For Graziella, of course

Before being the name of a painter,
of a great Cuban painter,
Pogolotti, in my childhood,
was a rustic road through undergrowth
which led to a big high house,
long and deep,
with a patio enclosed by wooden fencing
filled out by pumpkins and slow yagruma trees
and an exciting smell of goat in tomato and pepper
                                                    sauce.
In Pogolotti I spent so many Sundays
of okra under the mango trees,
of sugar and honey for new babies
of "don't go yet
Silvio is coming just now to see the girls".
Everything was singing at midday
when the chimneys of the small factories
were rising with their smoke
like a prayer against the elements
and hidden need.
Godmother was embracing me
and I looked at the unasphalted street
while the unemployed stevedores passed by,
the stevedores whipped by the industrial whistle
        of the ferry on the docks.
As in the Mexican murals
the air made thorns of itself,

las aguas hervían en un fastuoso plenilunio,
el plomo de los torneros caía en el alma
como una sangre desplomada al vacío.
De pronto, muchos años después,
aquellas chimeneas,
aquellos músculos selváticos,
se dieron a la fuga para siempre
y fueron encontrados,
infinitos domingos después,
en los cuadros de Don Marcelo,
adormecidos en su vigilia soñadora,
en mi infancia lejana,
entre la vanguardia y las aulas,
entre Marinetti y Prévert,
entre el pasillo umbroso de un museo
y el patio de los chivos.

Paisaje célebre

the waters boiled in a sumptuous full moon,
the lead of the lathe operators fell into the soul
like a blood collapsed into emptiness.
Of a sudden, many years later,
those chimneys,
those jungle muscles
gave themselves up to flight forever
and were found
infinite Sundays later,
in the paintings of Don Marcelo,
asleep in their dreamy vigil,
in my distant childhood,
between the vanguard and the classrooms,
between Marinetti and Prévert,
between the shady corridor of a museum
and the patio of the goats.

Famous Landscape

El Hogar

Así es el hogar.

¿Suave brisa o manchas de alquitrán?
¿Pinchos de hielo o cálida magnesia?
¿Estertor o desidia?

Es un claro domingo del hogar,
donde ni la mañana, ni la tarde,
ni la noche y su ocaso se hacen indefinibles.
Es un domingo hijo de la naturaleza del hogar.
Ácido como un cítrico, es
un hogar de trabajos y lágrimas. Es
el domingo que se provee de tíos nostálgicos,
ahijados, pensamientos,
primos sin dimensión,
ayes, maledicencias.
El hogar sin recursos, de telaraña,
el hogar poco: el amargo,
el escaso, el sufrido, el penado,
el sin juguetes toscos o lujosos,
el sin lumbre para encender el fogón de carbones.
Es tan sólo un hogar para ahogar.
Un hogar que es el templo de un sano estibador:
Felipe o Fleitas o Candelario o Juan
-el suyo es un hogar muy hogar
de donde fueron desterrados los misales, las prédicas,
las promesas del paraíso celestial,
para poner en su lugar,

THE HOME

The home is like this.

Gentle breeze or tar stains?
Ice thorns or warm magnesium?
Death rattle or apathy?

It is a bright Sunday in the home
where neither the morning, nor the evening,
nor the night and its sunset become indefinable.
It is a Sunday, child of the nature of the home.
Acid like a citrus, it is
a home of chores and tears. It is
the Sunday which provides itself with nostalgic aunts
                                    and uncles,
godchildren, thoughts,
cousins without degree,
sighs, backbiting.
The home without resources, of spider's web,
the home with little: the bitter,
the scarce, the suffered, the endured,
one without toys, crude or luxurious,
one without a flame to light the coal fire.
It is only a home in which to drown.
A home which is the temple of a healthy stevedore:
Felipe or Fleitas or Candelario or Juan
- his is a home which is very much a home
from which the Missals, the prayers,
the promises of celestial paradise were exiled,
to put in their place,

anémonas,
pargos
y carnadas.
Ellos, seres del mar sin mar, hijos de Yemayá,
hechos de sacos, sogas, güinches,
cubiertas, grúas y ferries,
desde de sus casas roídas,
surcan el puerto que quisieran.
Volantes y banderas salen de sus bocas saladas.
Alameda de Paula, qué reposo su hogar,
qué placidez su carne, su vida por la Muerte,
qué instante de fatuo carnaval vivieron.

Octubre imprescindible

anemones,
red snapper
and bait.
They, beings of the sea without a sea, sons of Yemayá,
made of sacks, rope, winches,
decks, cranes and ferries,
from their dilapidated houses,
sail to whichever port they wish.
Banners and flags come out of their salty mouths.
Alameda de Paula, what repose in their home,
what placidity their flesh, their life for Death,
what an instant of fatuous carnival they experienced.

Indispensable October

FÁBULA DE ALBAÑIL

El retrato en la sala
y el *zun zun dambaé*
tras de la puerta.
Pobre Pedro murió.
Un buen día
se marchó la existencia,
oh la infiel,
entre arena y gravilla,
soga y paleta.

Vino tinto de su palabra,
marisco hervido de su suerte,
se marcharon con él,
calladitos y en fila,
asidos de la mano
para el viaje polar.
Los capullos de la matina
abrieron como nunca.
Mas el cielo de Pedro
mantuvo el mismo azul
en la fiereza del andamio
donde acababa su espalda peregrina,
tan dura como el ágata,
tan dulce como el verso sabido.
Pedro sube a lo inmenso
con ansias de verano
y gestos de caballero provisional.
Funeral de los mudos,
cuánta tinta del alma habré volcado

FABLE OF A BUILDER'S LABOURER

The portrait in the room
and the *zun zun dambaé*
behind the door.
Poor Pedro died.
One fine day
existence went away,
oh unfaithful,
between sand and gravel,
rope and trowel.

The red wine of his words,
the boiled shellfish of his lot,
went off with him,
quiet and in single file,
holding hands,
for the polar journey.
The buds of the morning
opened as never before.
But Pedro's sky
kept the same blue
in the fierceness of the scaffolding
where his pilgrim back used to end up,
as hard as the agate,
as sweet as the well-known verse.
Pedro is going up to the immense
with a longing for Summer
and the gestures of a provisional gentleman.
Funeral of the dumb,
how much ink of the soul will I have spilled

en el deseo de recrearte,
y fue imposible,
y así, de cualquier modo, un día
tu fábula se irá
pendiente aún de todas las consignas.

Octubre imprescindible

into the desire to recreate you,
and it was impossible,
and thus, in whatever way, one day
your fable will go away
still dependent on all the directives.

Indispensable October

El Café

Mamá trae el café desde remotos mares
como si la historia de su vida
rondara cada frase de humo
que se entrelaza entre ella y yo.
Inusitada del amanecer, sonríe.
Y saltan sobre su cabello de azúcar
las pulseras de oro.
Y el hilo sobrio de su infancia
pervive entre las dos.

Quisiéramos un alto flamboyán de la montaña
a cuya justa sombra durmiese el trovador.

Piedra pulida

COFFEE

Mamma brings the coffee from remote seas
as if the history of her life
hung off every phrase of steam
which entwines itself between her and me.
Unused to the dawn, she smiles.
And the bracelets of gold
jump on her sugar hair.
And the sober thread of her childhood
Lives on between the two.

We would like a high flamboyant from the mountain
beneath whose neat shadow the troubadour might
                                                    sleep.

Polished Stone

COTORRA QUE ATRAVIESA MANRIQUE

A Chiqui Salsamendi

De súbito, una cotorra mínima
va a desplazar su pico por la calle Manrique
y la despavorida, ronronea, dando palos de ciego,
tal vez buscando algún destino.
Los verdes y los azules de su cuello
estallan frente a las zanahorias,
el berro y las lechugas.
Dos negras se aproximan,
desde la multitud,
en un vaivén de hamacas vivas,
columpiadas por el viento del Golfo.
Un vendedor de periódicos
apenas puede pregonar,
absorto ante el fulgor de la cotorra
y la belleza natural de las negras.
La calle Manrique es un boceto de Landaluze
y se detuvo el vendedor
como alguien que acaba de descubrir todo un
                                        zoológico.

Paisaje célebre

Budgerigar Crossing Manrique

To Chiqui Salsamendi

Suddenly, a tiny budgerigar
goes to take its beak for a walk along Manrique Street
and the terrified thing, chirps, striking out blindly
perhaps looking for some destination.
The greens and the blues of its neck
explode against the carrots,
the watercress and the lettuces.
Two black women approach,
out of the crowd,
in a rising and falling of living hammocks,
blown up and down by the wind from the Gulf.
A newspaper seller
is barely able to cry out
absorbed by the brilliance of the budgerigar
and the natural beauty of the black women.
Manrique Street is a sketch by Landaluze
and the seller stopped
like someone who has just discovered a whole zoo.

Famous Landscape

INSTANTE

Ayer, ella no comprendió las matemáticas
pero leyó con gusto una historia de África
donde contaban cosas
de tráfico y galeones.
Hoy, él fundó una novena para jugar pelota
y donó sangre en el hospitalito provincial.
Ella corrió toda una pista
y él fue a comprar almejas deliciosas
en un mercado.
Él soñaba con indias lavando todas a la orilla del río.
Ella fue a la nevera
y, con un placer casi prohibido,
devoró las almejas que él había conseguido
en el mercado.
Son las cuatro y diez de la tarde.
Ambos están mirando el mismo lente
y han compartido la misma esperanza.

Paisaje célebre

INSTANT

Yesterday, she didn't understand mathematics
but she read with pleasure a story of Africa
in which things were recounted
about traffic and galleons.
Today, he set up a nine to play ball
and gave blood in the little provincial hospital.
She ran a whole race
and he went to buy delicious clams
at a market.
He was dreaming about Indian women all washing
                  on the bank of the river.
She went to the fridge
and, with an almost forbidden pleasure,
devoured the clams which he had obtained
at the market.
It is ten past four in the afternoon
They are both looking into the same lens
and have shared the same hope.

Famous Landscape

EL RÍO DE MARTÍN PÉREZ

Casi a punto de perder un idioma,
miro el río de Martín Pérez,
minúscula corriente
ante la cual quiero postrarme
para alcanzar aires estables,
llegados del océano;
pero transcurren rastras y más rastras
y hay ciclos y panelitos y autobuses
bordados con un fango que forma un encaje
                                    republicano
y una guagua con cintas de colores
como las chimeneas de Luyanó aullando
contra las nubes vampiras del
Paso Superior. Río Martín Pérez,
vuelvo a mirarte
para rescatar tus aguas pocas
de un pasado en que sólo eras eso:
agua que viene y va.
Pasan los yerberos
con sombreros de picos,
sombreros esmirriados por las luces del sol,
sombreros de yarey sin raíces.
Pasan los ñáñigos con sus sacos gigantes
cargados de bledo y verdolaga,
palo vencedor,
hierbamora y muralla.

La estrella de la tarde
cae sobre sus cuerpos negros
como la noche que se avecina.

THE RIVER OF MARTIN PÉREZ

Almost on the point of losing a language,
I look at the river of Martin Pérez,
minuscule current
in front of which I wish to prostrate myself
to reach stable air,
come from the ocean;
but carts and more carts pass
and there are bikes and vans and buses
embroidered in a mud which forms a republican lace
and a bus with coloured ribbons
like the chimneys of Luyanó howling
against the vampire clouds of the
Paso Superior. Martin Pérez River,
I look at you again
to rescue your scarce waters
of a past in which you were only that:
water which comes and goes.
The field workers pass by
with peaked caps,
caps worn threadbare in the light of the sun,
caps of rootless yarey palm.
The *ñáñigos* with their giant sacks pass by
loaded with Swiss chard and purslane,
palo vencedor,
lemon verbena and *muralla*.

The evening star
falls on their black bodies
like the night which comes closer.

A punto de enloquecer junto a ti
estoy oliendo un fuego pordiosero
plantado en el corazón de la manigua,
como una reverencia inoportuna
en medio de tanta claridad
y tanta agua pequeña
abarcándolo todo sin devolvernos nada,
arrastrando en su curso
frágiles granos de maíz,
cabezas huecas de carneros,
plumas de pavoreal,
ojos de gallo viudo
y brebajes del cielo.
Río Martín Pérez que no apareces en las cartografías,
ni en ningún mapamundi;
río de mi pobreza líquida,
río de mi fortuna sólida
y de mi lengua cortada en dos;
río de mi familia sudorosa
y diezmada,
río de nuestras hambres
y de nuestra intranquilidad.

Río Martín Pérez, déjame cruzar.
Déjame llegar a Vertemati,
al palacio yoruba que apenas tiene techo
ni paredes. Sólo helechos transpirando en la humedad
de las alturas.
Allí necesito la risa de todos sus negros
y todas las negras,
las heridas de Antonio Maceo,
la flor punzó de Toussaint Louverture

On the point of going mad beside you
I smell a beggar fire
planted in the heart of the swamp,
like an inopportune reverence
in the middle of so much clarity
and so much shallow water
embracing it all without giving us anything back,
dragging in its path
fragile maize seeds,
hollow rams' heads,
peacock feathers,
widowed cocks' eyes
and magic potions from the heavens.
Martin Pérez River who do not appear on the maps,
nor in any mapamundi;
river of my liquid poverty,
river of my solid fortune,
and of my tongue cut in two,
river of my sweaty and decimated
family,
river of our famines
and of our unquietness.

Martin Pérez River, let me cross.
Let me get to Vertemati,
to the Yoruba palace which has hardly any roof
or walls. Only ferns transpiring in the humidity
of the heights.
There I need the laughter of all its black men
and all its black women,
the wounds of Antonio Maceo,
the bright red flower of Toussaint Louverture

en el castillo de Joux
y todo el parasol de Juan Gualberto Gómez.
Yo necesito tu otra orilla
en donde están seguramente todos mis sueños
                                    entamados;
río de mis dolores y mis penas,
río pequeñito como las historias de güijes
que caben en mi dedo meñique.
Río de aguas ningunas
que no estás en ningún grabado de Durnford
pero que te miran ciertos astros y todos los planetas.

Una guinea va alzando vuelo sobre un claro.

La quinta de los molinos

in Joux castle
and all of the parasol of Juan Gualberto Gómez.
I need your other bank
in which surely all my dreams are piled up;
river of my suffering and my pain,
tiny little river like the stories of *güijes*
which fit in my small finger.
River of no waters
who are in no engraving by Durnford
but some stars and all the planets look on you.

A guinea fowl is flying up over a clearing.

The Qunita de los Molinos

PERSONA

Cuál de estas mujeres soy yo?
¿O no soy yo la que está hablando
tras los barrotes de una ventana sin estilo
que da a la plenitud de todos estos siglos?
¿Acaso seré yo la mujer negra y alta
que corre y casi vuela
y alcanza records astronómicos,
con sus oscuras piernas celestiales
en su espiral de lunas?
¿En cuál músculo suyo se dibuja mi rostro,
clavado allí como un endecasílabo importado
de un país de nieve prohibida?

Estoy en la ventana
y cruza "la mujer de Antonio"[1];
"la vecinita de enfrente"[2], de una calle sin formas;
"la madre –negra Paula Valdés–."[3]
¿Quién es el señorito que sufraga
sus ropas y sus viandas
y los olores de vetiver ya desprendidos de su andar?
¿Qué permanece en mí de esa mujer?
¿Qué nos une a las dos? ¿Qué nos separa'?
¿O seré yo la "vagabunda del alba"[4],
que alquila taxis en la noche de los jaguares
como una garza tendida en el pavimento
después de haber sido cazada
        y esquilmada
        y revendida
por la Quinta de los Molinos

PERSON

Which of these women am I?
Am I not the one who is talking
through the bars of a nondescript window
which gives onto the plenitude of all these centuries?
Could I be the tall and black woman
who runs and almost flies
and sets astronomical records,
with her dark celestial legs
in her spiral of moons?
In which muscle of hers is my face drawn,
nailed there like an hendecasyllable imported
from a country of forbidden snow?

I am at the window
and "Antonio's wife"[1] is passing;
"the little woman across the way"[2], in a formless street;
"the mother –black Paula Valdés-."[3]
Who is the gentleman who defrays
her clothes and her food
and the scent of vetiver now given off as she walks?
What remains of me in that woman?
What unites the two of us? What separates us?
Or could I be the "vagabond of dawn"[4],
who hires taxis in the night of the jaguars
like a heron stretched on the pavement
after being hunted
         and clipped
         and touted
around the Quinta de los Molinos

y los embarcaderos del puerto?
Ellas: ¿quiénes serán? ¿o soy yo misma?
¿Quiénes son éstas que se parecen tanto a mí
no sólo por los colores de sus cuerpos
sino por ese humo devastador
que exhala nuestra piel de res marcada
por un extraño fuego que no cesa?
¿Por qué soy yo? ¿Por qué son ellas?

¿Quién es esa mujer
que está en todas nosotras huyendo de nosotras,
huyendo de su enigma y de su largo origen
con una incrédula plegaria entre los labios
o con un himno cantado
después de una batalla siempre renacida?

Todos mis huesos, ¿serán míos?
¿de quién serán todos mis huesos?
¿Me los habrán comprado
en aquella plaza remota de Gorée?
¿Toda mi piel será la mía
o me han devuelto a cambio
los huesos y la piel de otra mujer
cuyo vientre ha marcado otro horizonte,
otro ser, otras criaturas, otro dios?

Estoy en la ventana.
Yo sé que hay alguien.
Yo sé que una mujer ostenta mis huesos y mi carne;
que me ha buscado en su gastado seno
y que me encuentra en la vicisitud y el extravío.

and the jetties of the port?
They: who could they be? Or is it I myself?
Who are these women who seem so much like me
not only by the colour of their bodies
but by that devastating smoke
which our skin of livestock branded
by a strange fire which does not end exhales?
Why do I exist? Why do they?

Who is that woman
who is in all of us fleeing from us,
fleeing from her enigma and her long origin
with an incredulous prayer on her lips
or with an anthem sung
after a battle constantly reborn?

All my bones, are they mine?
whose could all my bones be?
Have they been bought for me
in that remote square in Gorée?
Is all my skin mine
or have I been given back in exchange
the bones and the skin of another woman
whose womb has marked another horizon,
another being, other children, another god?

I am at the window.
I know there is someone.
I know that a woman is showing off my bones and
                                          my flesh;
that she has looked for me in her spent breast
and that she finds me in vicissitude and in loss.

La noche está enterrada en nuestra piel.
La sabia noche recompone sus huesos y los míos.
Un pájaro del cielo ha trocado su luz en nuestros ojos.

La quinta de los molinos

[1 & 2] La mujer de Antonio y la vecinita de enfrente son
alusiones a personajes populares de un célebre son
de Miguel Matamoros, "La mujer de Antonio".
[3] Verso del poema "Quirino con su tres", de Nicolás
Guillén.
[4] Verso del poeta cubano Fayad Jamis.

Night is interred in our skin.
The wise night reconstitutes her bones and mine.
A bird from the sky has changed its light in our eyes.

The Qunita de los Molinos

1 & 2   Antonio's wife and the little woman from across the way are allusions to popular characters in a famous son by Miguel Matamoros, "La mujer de Antonio".

3   A line from the poem "Quirino con su tres", by Nicolás Guillén.

4   A line by the Cuban poet, Fayad Jamís.

MUJER NEGRA

Todavía huelo la espuma del mar que me hicieron
atravesar.
La noche, no puedo recordarla.
Ni el mismo océano podría recordarla.
Pero no olvido al primer alcatraz que divisé.
Altas, las nubes, como inocentes testigos presenciales.
Acaso no he olvidado ni mi costa perdida, ni mi
lengua ancestral.
Me dejaron aquí y aquí he vivido.
Y porque trabajé como una bestia,
aquí volví a nacer.
A cuanta epopeya mandinga intenté recurrir.

Me rebelé.

Su Merced me compró en una plaza.
Bordé la casaca de Su Merced y un hijo macho le
parí.
Mi hijo no tuvo nombre.
Y Su Merced, murió a manos de un impecable *lord*
inglés.

Anduve.

Esta es la tierra donde padecí bocabajos y azotes.
Bogué a lo largo de todos sus ríos.

BLACK WOMAN

Still I smell the foam of the sea which they made me
cross.
The night, I cannot remember it.
Not even the ocean itself could remember it.
But I do not forget the first gannet I made out.
High, the clouds, like innocent eyewitnesses.
Perhaps I have not forgotten either my lost coast, or
my ancestral tongue.
They left me here and here I have lived.
And because I worked like a beast,
here I was born again.
To how many Mandinga epopeias did I try to have
recourse.

I rebelled.

His Honour bought me in a square.
I embroidered His Honour's coat and gave birth to a
son for him.
My son had no name.
And His Honour, he died at the hands of an
impeccable English lord.

I walked.

This is the land in which I suffered beatings and
floggings.
I rowed the length of all its rivers.

Bajo su sol sembré, recolecté y las cosechas no comí.
Por casa tuve un barracón.
Yo misma traje piedras para edificarlo,
pero canté al natural compás de los pájaros nacionales.

Me sublevé.

En esta misma tierra toqué la sangre húmeda
y los huesos podridos de muchos otros,
traídos a ella, o no, igual que yo.
Ya nunca más imaginé el camino a Guinea.
¿Era a Guinea? ¿A Benin? ¿Era a Madagascar? ¿O a
        Cabo Verde?

Trabajé mucho más.

Fundé mejor mi canto milenario y mi esperanza.
Aquí construí mi mundo.

Me fui al monte.

Mi real independencia fue el palenque
y cabalgué entre las tropas de Maceo.

Sólo un siglo más tarde,
junto a mis descendientes,
desde una azul montaña,

Under its sun I sowed, I reaped and I did not eat the
                                                harvests.
For a house I had a shack
I myself brought stones to build it.
but I sang to the natural beat of the national birds.

        I rose up.

In this same land I touched the humid blood
and the rotted bones of many others,
brought to it, or not, the same as I.
By then I did not imagine the way to Guinea any
                                                more.
Was it to Guinea? To Benin? Was it to Madagascar?
Or to
        Cape Verde?

        I worked much harder.

I laid better foundations for my millennial song and
                                                my hope.
Here I built my world.

        I went off to the mountains.

My real independence was the palenque
and I rode among the troops of Maceo.

Only a century later,
together with my descendants,
from a blue mountain,

bajé de la Sierra

para acabar con capitales y usureros,
con generales y burgueses.
Ahora soy: Sólo hoy tenemos y creamos.
Nada nos es ajeno.
Nuestra la tierra.
Nuestros el mar y el cielo.
Nuestras la magia y la quimera.
Iguales míos, aquí los veo bailar
alrededor del árbol que plantamos para el comunismo.
Su pródiga madera ya resuena.

Parajes de una época

I came down from the Sierra

to put an end to capitalists and usurers,
to generals and bourgeois.
Now I am: Only today do we have and create.
Nothing is outside our reach.
Ours the land.
Ours the sea and the sky.
Ours magic and the chimera.
My equals, here I watch them dance
around the tree we planted for communism.
Its prodigious wood already resounds.

Places in a Time

Glossary

Abel Santamaría (1925-1953) is one of the legendary heroes of the Cuban Revolution which triumphed on the first of January 1959. After the assault on the Moncada Barracks, which took place on July 26th 1953, Abel was tortured and massacred. His torturers took out his eyes and subsequently, in an attempt to gain information, showed them to his sister Haydée, who also took part in the assault, through the bars of the prison in Santiago de Cuba where she was being detained. (NM)

Alameda de Paula is one of the most enchanting avenues in Havana. Not very extensive, it stretches along the docks where my father worked as a stevedore. Often, on Sundays, he would take me for a walk along it. (NM)

Baas: Master in Afrikaans, (or boss). (JA)

Bantustan: 10 territories called bantustans were created as homelands, on the introduction of apartheid in South Africa, for the black population. These were organised on the basis of ethnic and linguistic groupings; for example, KwaZulu was the appointed homeland of the Zulu people, the Xhosa were assigned to Transkei and Ciskei. Though these homelands were officially designated states, they were essentially administrative regions created by the Apartheid government with the implicit objective of concentrating the black population in overpopulated, poorly serviced and agriculturally barren lands. (JA)

Blaise Cendrars (Fréderic-Louis Sauser, 1887-1961), Swiss-born French poet and novelist. Innovative as a poet, with a biography as artfully fictionalised as his writing, he produced novels which were a mixture of reportage, science fiction, historical fact and autobiography. (JA)

Bledo (Swiss chard), verdolaga (purslane), palo vencedor, hierbamora (lemon verbena) and muralla are all herbs which, in themselves, have curative or supernatural powers, as stipulated in certain Cuban ritual ceremonies. (NM)

Camilo Cienfuegos (1932-1959) was one of the most popular guerillas in the armed struggle on the Sierra Maestra unleashed in 1956 against the military dictatorship of Fulgencio Batista. His men and those of Che Guevara joined up to take the city of Santa Clara, together opening the way towards definitive liberation. Camilo, with his big hat, and Che, with his black beret, today constitute a beautiful symbol of liberty for young people of the whole planet. (NM)

Changó or shango. Main orisha of fire, lightning, thunder and war, syncretised with the Catholic St Barbara. (Pérez Sarduy/Stubbs)

Chinos. When Spanish colonisation began, Cuba was populated by the Siboney and Taíno peoples. These indigenous peoples were virtually exterminated by a combination of marauding conquistadors, common and relatively innocuous European diseases unknown in the Caribbean until then, and slavery, which none of the indigenous populations of Latin America subjected to it survived. With the development of sugar plantations and refineries in the mid-seventeenth-century the importation of black slaves from Africa was rapidly expanded and continued until 1821 when the trafficking of slaves across the Atlantic was prohibited by treaty. Although Spain did not finally abolish slavery in its dominions until the period 1880-86, after 1821 there was a growing need to look elsewhere for cheap labour as the slave population had never reproduced itself at a rate sufficient to cope with the exponentially growing demand which continued on the plantations throughout the nineteenth century. Two experiments were tried in Cuba mid century: the importation of Mexican Indians from the Yucatán peninsula, promptly deemed a failure as the Indians proved no more able to survive the harsh conditions than their forebears; and, more long-lasting and of greater demographic impact in Cuba, the contracting of indentured labour from China and the Portuguese colony of Macao. The first Chinese arrived in 1847. 132,435 came in total between 1853 and 1873. The Chinese did not intermarry and retain to this day a visible cultural and ethnic presence in Cuba. See Napoleon Seuc, "Los chinos de Cuba" in *La enciclopedia de Cuba*, Vol. 6, 2nd Ed., Prosa de

Guerra, Sociedad, Filosofía. San Juan and Madrid: Enciclopedia y Clásicos Cubanos Inc., 1977. (JA)

Cimarrón, a maroon or runaway slave. (Pérez Sarduy/Stubbs)

Danzón, a dance popular among slaves in the nineteenth century adapted from formal European modes of the time. (JA)

Dessalines, Jean-Jacques (c.1758-1806): Along with Toussaint L'Ouverture and Alexander Pétion, -all of them with tragic destinies- he is one of the founders of the Haitian nation. (NM) Dessalines was born in Guinea and imported into Haiti as a slave, assuming the name of his French planter master. He was second only to Toussaint in the slave revolt of 1791. After the former's arrest in 1802, Dessalines renewed the war against the French and forced them to evacuate Haiti in 1803. He declared Haitian independence in 1804 and was crowned Emperor Jean Jacques I on 8th October 1804. Two years later, having alienated many of his erstwhile supporters, he died trying to suppress a rebellion, cut down by his successor Henri Christophe. (JA)

Durnford, Elias, English engraver: His engravings are fundamental to the history of the art in Cuba in the nineteenth-century. (NM).

El Olonés: The French buccaneer, Nau, known as El Olonés, was, sadly, famous because of his predatory activities in and around various Caribbean islands in the seventeenth century. (NM)

Eleggua or elegba, legba or elegbara: Main orisha, opens the path for other orishas, who can take 21 different paths: alagguan, alona, babalarube, lubaniba, muñunga, nkyuyu; syncretised with the Catholic St Anthony. (Pérez Sarduy/Stubbs)

Gorée island, major slave trading port, off Dakar, in what is now Senegal. (JA)

Gregorio Valdés was a Cuban primitive painter who passed long periods in Florida, especially in Tampa and Key West. I discovered his painting through a beautiful essay by the English poet Elizabeth Bishop. (NM)

Guardiero or warder: In the slave plantations, the owners established the practice of choosing the oldest of the elder slaves to watch over the paltry sleep of his fellows. He was a type of overseer in charge of the slaves' domestic life, when they returned from the heavy work in the plantation. (NM)

Güijes: A fictional character in the popular imagination which appeared frequently in the work of those who cultivated AfroCuban poetry. Emilio Ballegas defines them thus: "A jigüe or river spirit [...] The güijes do mischievous things to passers-by and carry off children who swim in rivers without their parents' consent. Jigües are dwarves according to tradition [...]. They are imagined as dwarves, with bug ears and a large stomach. They are black." In Emilio Ballagas, *Mapa de la poesía negra americana*, ilus de D. Ravenet. Buenos Aires: Pleamar, 1946, p. 307. (NM)

Iruque is an instrument of Oy, the goddess of the winds, death and graveyards in Cuban santería. It is made from horse hair and the goddess raises it to show her power. (Pérez Sarduy/Stubbs)

Joux: Fort de Joux, 3,000 feet up in the Jura mountains in France, built at the time of the Crusades on top of a rocky summit, 500 feet high, and covered in snow for 8 months of the year, it is the place where Toussaint L'Ouverture was imprisoned by the French from August 1802 to his death in April 1803. Though he was not formally sentenced to death, his end was almost certainly brought about by calculated neglect, gradual sensory and physical deprivation and, for such a denizen of the tropics, the unbearably cold climate. See Wenda Parkinson, "*This Gilded African*": *Toussaint L'Ouverture*. London, Melbourne and New York: Quartet Books, 1978, pp. 195-207. (JA)

Jovellanos, a town in Matanzas province in Cuba.

Juan Gualberto Gómez, a great Cuban patriot, a tireless fighter against slavery and for the civil rights of the black and mulatto population of Cuba, he was a trusted aide of José Martí when he set up the foundations of the Cuban Revolutionary Party in preparation for the War of 1895. (NM)

Jutía, edible tropical rat.

Landaluze, Víctor Patricio de (1828-1889). Basque-born painter of reactionary political views who wrote newspaper articles in which he criticised any moves towards separation from Spain, he also produced political cartoons in the same vein, but, in his oils and watercolours, he captured Cuban life in all its colour and multi-racial complexity. His paintings are often categorised as costumbrista, a reference to a predominantly literary, Spanish nineteenth-century trend towards depicting highly accurate and detailed scenes from rural and urban working-class life in fiction. He painted many scenes of Havana life in the mid-nineteenth century. (JA)

Louisiana, originally a vast tranche of land covering an area which stretched along the great plains of the midwest of the United States, from the Rocky Mountains in the west almost to the Appalachians in the east, and from the Mississippi delta in the south to beyond the Great Lakes in the north, in what is today Canada. It was claimed in 1682 for the French government by Cavelier de la Salle. Most of the land west of the Mississippi was ceded to Spain in 1762, and the following year, the land east of the Mississippi was turned over to England, while France remained in control of a much smaller territory. In 1803, France sold its remaining possessions to the United States in the Louisiana Purchase. Under the French, indigo plantations were established from the 1720s on, cotton from 1740 and there were also some sugar plantations, all worked by black slaves.

Luyanó, a locality in Havana.

Maceo, Antonio (1845-1896). General Maceo, known as the Bronze Titan because of his stature as well as his military prowess, was the son of a free AfroCuban father and a free mulatta mother. His father belonged to a Masonic lodge in Santiago which had, for some time, been a hotbed of revolution and democratic and reform-minded thinking. Maceo joined, as a young man in 1864, and found himself, in 1867, in the midst of the revolutionary organisation in Eastern Cuba emanating from this lodge. The declaration known as the Grito de Yara in the following year of 1868 launched the first War of Independence which ended in

1878. In 1895, the Grito de Baire initiated the Second War of Independence which ultimately led to secession from Spain. Though the outbreak of the Spanish-American War hastened independence, finally achieved in 1898, it also hamstrung it, as Cuba remained under US occupation of Cuba from 1898 to 1903 and this set a pattern for Cuba-US relations until 1959. Acknowledged subsequently to be the great leader of the War of Independence, Maceo died, however, on 7th December 1896, mortally wounded in a minor skirmish in San Pedro, and, while he lived, he was subject to racist resentment on the part of the creole (ethnic Spanish) generals in the independence movement. Indeed, his death was welcomed with jubilation in certain quarters in the United States for overtly racist reasons. Anti-Independence factions in Cuba and Spain, however, confined their reactions to the purely military and political. In contrast, throughout most of Cuba, in Latin America and much of the rest of the then developed world, Maceo was mourned as the last great fighting captain of the century and a revolutionary leader of great stature. See Philip S. Forner, Antonio Maceo: "The Bronze Titan" of Cuba's Struggle for Independence. New York and London: *Monthly Review Press*, 1977. (JA)

Machado, Antonio (1875-1939). Spanish poet, philosopher and vociferous supporter of the defeated Republican government during the Spanish Civil War, whose most famous collection of poems, *Campos de Castilla* (*Castilian Fields*), published in 1912, is credited with epitomising the movement of certain major figures in Spanish literature away from a French-influenced esoteric decadence towards an exaltation of the plain values of a, somewhat idealised, Castilian (and therefore Spanish) landscape and peasantry. In the first line of the first poem of that collection, *Retrato* (Portrait) Machado states, "Mi infancia son recuerdos de un patio de Sevilla" (my infancy is memories of a patio in Seville). Nancy Morejón's allusion is, in her own words, obvious (*por supuesto*). (JA)

Majomía is a repetitive and whispered complaint or lament. (NM)

Manatí: The manatee is one of only two sirenian mammals, the other being the sea cow. They are found off the shores of the America, the Caribbean and Africa, have a prehensile upper lip and flattened tail, and look like whales. (JA) Furthermore, Fernando Ortiz adds: "As well as the animal of this name, a stick or whip made of its skin. The use of the manatí stick was forbidden in these Antilles during the slavery era, and it could not be used to flog slaves. It is said this was because it was very cruel. It may be supposed that this was due to the fact that the mark of its lash was permanent and that later made the sale of a slave more difficult, since the buyer would assume, on seeing the traces of punishment, that the unfortunate had the mark of being a turbulent character." In Fernando Ortiz, *Nuevo cataro de cubanismos*. Havana: Ciencias Sociales, 1974, p. 339. (NM)

Manrique, Jorge (1440?-1479). Spanish poet, courtier, politician and soldier, best known for a collection of exquisitely lyrical short poems, *coplas*, on the death, in 1476, of his father, a grand master of the military order of Santiago, the *Coplas de Don Jorge Manrique por la muerte de su padre*. (JA)

Marie-Galante: An island in the Guadeloupe archipelago. The first sugar-mill was set up on the island in 1664, only sixteen years after French colonisers arrived in 1648 and sugar was the reason for the importation of slaves onto the island over the next century and a half. See Christian Schnackenbourg, "Recherches sur l'histoire de l'industrie sucrière "Marie-Galante", Extrait du *Bulletin de la Societé d'Histoire de la Guadeloupe*, N°s 48-50, 2e-4e trimestres, 1981.

Marimbula: The marimbula produces a sound similar to that of the marimba but is a different instrument. Helio Orovio maintains that it is "an instrument used by son groups, in Cuba. It is said to derive from the African sansa or mbila, and has been observed in other countries of the Caribbean. It is made of a hollow box with a hole over which steel strings are stretched and fastened in the centre, with the ends loose and raised, so that when they are beaten they produced vibrations in the sound box. The player sits over the box and makes sound by pressing the strings with the fingertips. It is used instead of a double base. Even though it may sometimes have five or up to seven strings, generally it plays the tonic, the dominant and the subdominant." In Helio Orovio, *Diccionario de la musica cubana: biogrfico y técnico*. Havana: Letras Cubanas, 1981, p.237. (NM) The marimbula is made of wickerwork and usually used to accompany the congo drums. (JA)

Marinetti, Emilio Filippo Tommaso (1876-1944). Born in Alexandria, Italian writer and one of the founders of Futurism. He glorified war, the machine age, speed and dynamism and condemned all traditional forms of literature and art. (JA)

Martí, José Julián (1853-1895). Journalist, poet, essayist, diplomat, revolutionary, the intellectual power behind Cuban Independence and a pioneer of thinking on race equality. He founded the Cuban Revolutionary Party in 1892, and, fighting in the War of Independence in 1895, was killed in a skirmish near Dos Ríos. (JA)

Martín Pérez is the name of a working-class district on the outskirts of Havana. (NM)

Maurice Bishop (d.1983). Leader of the Grenadian revolution (1979-83) and Prime Minister in charge of the socialist People's Revolutionary Government in 1983, he was ousted in a coup by Bernard Coard, the leader of the New Jewel Movement, a partner in government, and executed in suspicious circumstances with three of his ministers in Fort Rupert on 19th October. Bishop had aligned Grenada with Cuba and he was respected by Fidel Castro who, in contrast, called Coard "the Pol Pot of the Caribbean". Castro subsequently sent Cuban reservists to fight on the Grenadian side against the Americans during the invasion which was prompted, in part, by the coup and the execution of Bishop. The following statistics provide an idea of the level of Cuban involvement in the conflict: 45 Grenadians died and 396 were wounded, 24 Cubans died and 59 were wounded and 18 Americans died and 118 were wounded. When Bishop died he was widely mourned in Cuba. See Eric Nabajoth, "L'influence cubaine dans la Caraibe, Mythe et Realité: Le cas de Grenade" in *Cuba et les Antilles; Actes du Colloque de Pointe*-à-Pitre (3-5 décembre 1984), Preface, Alain Yacou. Talence: Presses Universitaires de Bordeaux, 1988, pp.182-3. (JA)

Maroon, the Caribbean name for a runaway slave. (Pérez Sarduy/ Stubbs)

Muralla, see bledo.

Ñáñigo, practitioner of ñáñiguismo, that is membership of a male secret society, abaku, founded in Havana in the nineteenth century by Africans of Calabar. (Pérez Sarduy/Stubbs)

Nieves Fresneda was the most gifted exponent of Cuban traditional dance. Her dance for Yemayá was a prodigy in itself. She died in Havana in 1981. (NM)

Ochún or oshun, the main orisha of sexuality, goddess of rivers and springs, can take various forms as in ochún kolé. (Pérez Sarduy/ Stubbs)

Olofi, supreme orisha, eternal father. (Pérez Sarduy/Stubbs)

Orisha, god in santería (Pérez Sarduy/Stubbs)

Palenque: An enclosed dwelling in the mountains where escaped slaves gathered and attempted to recreate African tribal tradition and the tribal way of life. (NM) Maroons often lived in organised bands in the mountains and periodically came down to pillage and steal from settlements and plantations. These settlements were called quilombos in Brazil and were established all over Central and Latin America practically since slavery began. Now they have almost uniformly disappeared, with the possible exceptions of the Bush Negroes of Surinam and the Black Caribs of Dominica and Central America. See Herbert S. Klein, *African Slavery in Latin America and the Caribbean*. New York and Oxford: OUP, 1986, pp. 200-04. (JA)

Palo vencedor, see bledo.

Pogolotti, Marcelo (1902-1988): Cuban artist who spent less than ten years of his life as a painter. On his return from France in 1930 he painted working class scenes in the tubular style of Léger. Subsequently he became a surrealist and, when he lost his sight, he devoted himself to literature and art criticism. (JA)

Prévert, Jacques (1900-1977). French poet and screenwriter, many of his poems were set as cabaret songs and achieved great popularity. He also wrote the screenplays for successful and well-known films such as *Les enfants du paradis* (1945) and *Les portes de la nuit* (1946). (JA)

Rebambaramba is a very colloquial and popular Cuban expression meaning a lot of noise, pandemonium, a commotion. Alejo Carpentier wrote the libretto for a famous ballet called *La rebambaramba*, with music by the Cuban composer, Amadeo Roldn. (NM)

San Francisco de Paula is a small village on the outskirts of Havana. During his time in Cuba, in the fifties, the writer Ernest Hemingway lived in a house there which is today an attractive museum. (NM)

Toussaint L'Ouverture, Pierre François Dominique (1746-1803). Born of African slave parents in Haiti, Toussaint was freed in 1777, joined the black revolutionary insurgents in 1791, and was named commander-in-chief on the island by the French Convention in 1797. He drove the French and Spanish out of Haiti and presided over the abolition of slavery in 1801 only to have Napoleon decree its restoration. Thereafter he and his confederates sought full independence from France but they were overpowered by superior imperial forces and Toussaint was imprisoned in the fortress of Joux in France in August 1802. He died less than a year later, in April 1803, of studied French neglect. (JA)

Vertemati is the name of a street in Guanabacoa, a city on the edge of Havana province, well known for its wide range of AfroCuban culture. Great Cuban musicians such as Ernesto Lecuona, Rita Montaner and Bola de Nieve were born in Guanabacoa. (NM)

Wounded Knee or Chankpe Opi Wakpala to give it its indigenous name, a creek in South Dakota. In 1890, the last Sioux chief, Big Foot, and his people surrendered themselves and their arms to the US army after the death of Sitting Bull and the virtual end of the Sioux War. They were escorted by the army back to their reservation but there was, inevitably, a lot of tension and mistrust on the journey back, despite all the ailing Big Foot's efforts to keep the situation calm. When they stopped for rest at Wounded Knee, in the height of winter, it is believed that one of the soldiers thought he saw a Sioux brave raising a weapon and opened fire, precipitating a massacre of unarmed men, women and children. (JA)

Yemayá, the main orisha of the sea and motherhood, sister of ochún. (Pérez Sarduy/Stubbs)

Zunzun dambaé is a tiny bird native to our countryside, in appearance reminiscent of a hummingbird. This ritornello alludes to those remains of African words which appear in prayers and songs brought by the slaves to Cuba. Fábula de albañil (Fable of a Builder's Labourer) refers to the words of an old song which the people used to sing and which was very popular at the beginning of the fifties. It is said that it was recovered, in Guanabacoa, thanks to the memory of Inés Fernández, the mother of the pianist, composer and singer Ignacio Villa, known throughout the world as Bola de Nieve (Snowball). Raquel Villa, Bola's sister, confirmed this for me. (NM)

Biographical Notes

Nancy Morejón (Havana, 1944), one of the most relevant voices in contemporary Cuban poetry, has been awarded special recognition within and outside our continent, especially in Mexico, Venezuela and the United States. A translator and essayist as well, she published her first book in 1962 and the most recent, *La quinta de los molinos* (*The Mills Farm*), in 2000. The previous collection to that, *Elogio y paisaje* (*Eulogy and Landscape*), won the Critics Prize in 1997. Her published work includes more than twelve titles, among which *Richard trajo su flauta y otros argumentos* (*Richard Brought his Flute and Other Stories*) (1967), *Where the Island Sleeps Like a Wing* (Bilingual Anthology, 1985), *Piedra pulida* (*Polished Stone*) (1986), and *Botella al mar* (*Bottle in the Sea*) brought out by the Spanish publisher Olifante, stand out. She is an expert on the work of Nicolás Guillén and the arts in the Caribbean. Member of the jury for the Carbet del Caribe Prize. Member of the Cuban Academy of Language. The University of Howard, Washington DC, published a collection of critical studies of her work edited by Professor Miriam De Costa-Willis, entitled *Singular Like a Bird: The Art of Nancy Morejón*. The Madrid publisher, Visor, recently brought out an anthology, *Richard trajo su flauta y otros poemas* (*Richard Brought His Flute and Other Poems*), edited by Mario Benedetti. She is a member of the Advisory Council of the National Theatre of Cuba. At present she is director of the Centre for Caribbean Studies of the Casa de las Américas.

Jean Andrews was born in the west of Ireland and currently teaches in the Department of Hispanic and Latin American Studies at the University of Nottingham. Her most recent academic publications are on nineteenth century opera and post-colonial narrative and she has also just translated Sor Juana Inés de la Cruz's *Allegorical Neptune* (1680) for the Europa Triumphans Project.

OTHER TITLES
FROM
MANGO PUBLISHING

Leaves in the Wind *Selected Writings of Beryl Gilroy*
£12.99 (ISBN 1 902294 00 9)

Haunted by History *Poetry by Joan Anim-Addo*
£6.99 (ISBN 1 902294 03 3)

Another Doorway: Visible Inside the Museum
Poetry and Short Stories from the Caribbean Women Writers' Alliance
£6.00 (ISBN 1 902294 01 7)

Voice Memory Ashes: Lest We Forget
*Poetry and Short Stories Celebrating and Paying Homage
to the Collective Memory of Caribbean Experience*
£6.00 (ISBN 1 902294 04 1)

A Way to Catch the Dust *Short Stories by Jacob Ross*
£8.99 (ISBN 1 902294 08 4)

Windrush to Lewisham: 'Memoirs of Uncle George'
by W. George Brown
£6.00 (ISBN 1 902294 07 6)

The Best Philosophers I Know Can't Read and Write
Poetry by Velma Pollard
£7.99 (ISBN 1 902294 10 6)

Mango Publishing
PO Box 13378, London SE27 0ZN